Table of Contents

INTRODUCTION
To Met Flex Diet

The Science Behind Metabolic Flexibility

Metabolic flexibility refers to the ability of an organism to efficiently switch between utilizing different fuel sources, primarily carbohydrates and fats, depending on the availability of these nutrients and the body's energy requirements. This metabolic adaptability is crucial for maintaining optimal health, body composition, and physical performance.

At the heart of metabolic flexibility is the balance between two metabolic states: glycolysis and lipolysis. Glycolysis is the process through which the body breaks down glucose (derived from carbohydrates) to produce energy in the form of ATP (adenosine triphosphate). On the other hand, lipolysis refers to the breakdown of stored body fat (triglycerides) into fatty acids, which can also be used as an energy source.

In a metabolically flexible individual, the body can efficiently transition between glycolysis and lipolysis based on the availability of carbohydrates and fats. For example, when carbohydrates are scarce or during periods of fasting, the body can readily switch to using fat as its primary fuel source. Conversely, when carbohydrates are abundant, the body can easily transition back to using glucose for energy.

The importance of metabolic flexibility lies in its potential health benefits, which include improved body composition, enhanced physical performance, better blood sugar control, and reduced risk of chronic diseases such as obesity, type 2 diabetes, and cardiovascular disease.

Factors that can influence metabolic flexibility include genetics, diet, physical activity, sleep, and stress. The Met Flex Diet, developed by Dr. Ian Smith, is designed to help individuals improve their metabolic flexibility by strategically incorporating carbohydrates, prioritizing protein intake, and balancing healthy fats in their daily diet. This dietary approach aims to optimize the body's ability to use different fuel sources efficiently, leading to better overall health and well-being.

Benefits of the Met Flex Diet

The Met Flex Diet, designed by Dr. Ian Smith, is a comprehensive dietary approach that focuses on improving metabolic flexibility.

This diet plan offers numerous health benefits, stemming from its ability to optimize the body's use of different fuel sources and promote overall well-being. Some key benefits of the Met Flex Diet include:

Improved body composition: By promoting metabolic flexibility, the Met Flex Diet helps the body become more efficient at burning stored fat for fuel. This can lead to a reduction in body fat percentage and an increase in lean muscle mass, resulting in a healthier and more toned physique.

Enhanced weight management: The Met Flex Diet encourages a balanced intake of macronutrients and incorporates principles of carb cycling, which can help regulate appetite and promote a healthier relationship with food. These factors can contribute to better weight management and long-term weight maintenance.

Better blood sugar control: By strategically incorporating carbohydrates and prioritizing protein intake, the Met Flex Diet can help stabilize blood sugar levels and reduce the risk of insulin resistance. This may lead to a lower risk of develop-ing type 2 diabetes and other blood sugar-related health issues.

Reduced risk of chronic diseases: By promoting a balanced and nutrient-dense diet, the Met Flex Diet can contribute to a lower risk of developing chronic diseases such as obesity, heart disease, and certain types of cancer.

Greater diet sustainability: The Met Flex Diet is not a restrictive eating plan, which means individuals can enjoy a variety of foods while still reaping the benefits of improved metabolic flexibility. This flexibility makes it easier to adhere to the diet in the long term, leading to lasting lifestyle changes and better overall health.

Personalized approach: The Met Flex Diet can be tailored to an individual's specific needs, preferences, and goals, making it a versatile and adaptable dietary plan that can suit various lifestyles and requirements.

Getting Started with the Met Flex Diet

To embark on your journey with the Met Flex Diet, follow these steps to set yourself up for success:

Educate yourself: Familiarize yourself with the principles and guidelines of the Met Flex Diet. Understand the importance of metabolic flexibility, the role of macronutrients, and the concept of carb cycling. This knowledge will empower you to make informed choices and adjustments as needed.

Assess your current eating habits: Take a close look at your current diet to identify areas for improvement. Consider tracking your food intake for a few days to get a better understanding of your macronutrient consumption, meal timing, and food choices.

Set realistic goals: Establish clear, attainable goals for your health, body composition, and performance. Be specific and set short-term and long-term targets that will help you stay motivated and focused on your progress.

Plan your meals: Create a meal plan that incorporates the principles of the Met Flex Diet, such as prioritizing protein intake, strategically incorporating carbohydrates, and balancing healthy fats. Make sure to include a variety of nutrient-dense whole foods to ensure you receive essential vitamins and minerals.

Prepare a shopping list: Based on your meal plan, prepare a shopping list that includes Met Flex Diet staples, such as lean proteins, whole grains, fruits and vegetables, healthy fats, and high-fiber foods.

Organize your kitchen: Set up your kitchen for success by stocking it with the necessary tools, appliances, and pantry staples that support your new eating habits. Remove or minimize the presence of processed, high-sugar, and unhealthy food options.

Meal prep: Dedicate time each week to preparing meals and snacks in advance. This will make it easier to stick to the Met Flex Diet guidelines and ensure you have healthy options readily available.

Track your progress: Regularly monitor your progress by taking note of changes in your body composition, energy levels, and overall well-being. Consider using a food diary, fitness app, or other tracking tools to help you stay accountable and make adjustments as needed.

Seek support: Share your goals with friends and family, or join online forums and social media groups focused on the Met Flex Diet. Engaging with others who share your interests can provide encouragement, motivation, and valuable insights.

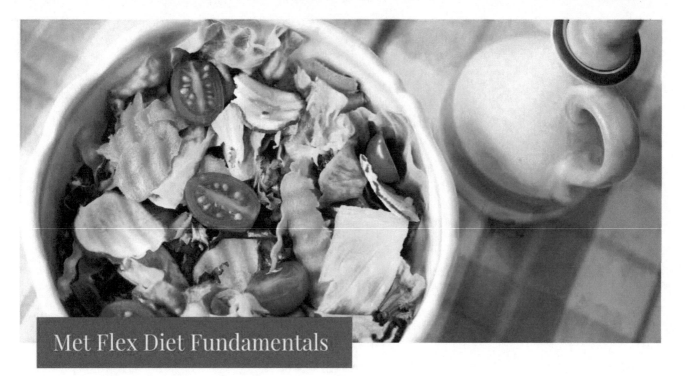

Understanding Macronutrients

Carbohydrates: These provide energy to the body, primarily in the form of glucose. In the Met Flex Diet, carbohydrates are strategically incorporated to support metabolic flexibility, with a focus on whole grains, fruits, and vegetables for their nutrient density and fiber content.

Proteins: These are the building blocks for muscles, organs, and various body tissues. In the Met Flex Diet, protein intake is prioritized to support muscle growth, recovery, and satiety. Lean sources of protein such as poultry, fish, legumes, and low-fat dairy are recommended.

Fats: These are essential for hormone production, nutrient absorption, and overall health. In the Met Flex Diet, a balance of healthy fats is emphasized, with a focus on monounsaturated and polyunsaturated fats from sources like avocados, nuts, seeds, and olive oil.

Eating for Metabolic Flexibility

Incorporating carbohydrates strategically: Carbohydrates are included in the Met Flex Diet based on individual needs and activity levels. Carb cycling is a key component, with higher-carb days interspersed with lower-carb days to enhance metabolic flexibility.

Prioritizing protein intake: Ensuring adequate protein consumption is crucial for maintaining lean muscle mass and promoting satiety. The Met Flex Diet recommends consuming a source of protein with every meal and snack.

Balancing healthy fats: Healthy fats are essential for overall health and well-being. The Met Flex Diet encourages the consumption of monounsaturated and polyunsaturated fats while minimizing the intake of unhealthy trans and saturated fats.

Meal Timing and Frequency

Meal spacing: Distributing meals evenly throughout the day can help maintain consistent energy levels and support metabolic flexibility. The Met Flex Diet generally recommends consuming 3 main meals and 1-2 snacks per day.

Fasting and metabolic flexibility: Intermittent fasting can be a valuable tool for enhancing metabolic flexibility. However, it's not a requirement of the Met Flex Diet and should be approached based on individual preferences and needs.

Snacking guidelines: Snacks can help manage hunger and maintain energy levels between meals. The Met Flex Diet recommends choosing nutrient-dense, high-protein snacks to support metabolic flexibility.

Hydration and Supplements

The importance of hydration: Staying well-hydrated is crucial for overall health, including metabolic flexibility. The Met Flex Diet recommends consuming at least 8 cups (64 ounces) of water daily or more, depending on individual needs and activity levels.

Recommended supplements for the Met Flex Diet: While it's possible to obtain most nutrients through a balanced diet, some individuals may benefit from supplements such as multivitamins, omega-3 fatty acids, vitamin D, or protein powder. Consult with a healthcare professional before adding supplements to your routine.

By adhering to these fundamental principles, you can optimize your metabolic flexibility and reap the numerous health benefits of the Met Flex Diet.

TIPS & GUIDANCE
for Successes

MEAL PREP STRATEGIES

Meal prepping is an effective way to stay on track with the Met Flex Diet and ensure that you always have healthy, balanced meals available. Here are some meal prep strategies to help you succeed:

PLAN AHEAD

Create a meal plan for the week, taking into account your macronutrient needs, higher-carb and lower-carb days, and any dietary preferences or restrictions. A well-thought-out meal plan will make grocery shopping and meal prepping more efficient.

DEVELOP A SHOPPING LIST

Based on your meal plan, make a shopping list that includes all necessary ingredients. Organize the list by sections of the grocery store to make shopping quicker and more efficient.

FREEZE EXTRAS

Prepare meals that can be frozen and reheated later, such as soups, stews, or casseroles. This is a great way to have healthy options on hand for days when you don't have time to cook.

ALLOCATE MEAL PREP TIME

Set aside dedicated time each week to prepare meals and snacks. This could be a single block of time on the weekend or smaller blocks of time throughout the week, depending on your schedule and preferences.

USE VERSATILE INGREDIENTS

Choose ingredients that can be easily repurposed for different meals. For example, cook a large batch of shredded chicken that can be used in salads, wraps, or stir-fries throughout the week.

PRE-PORTION MEALS

Divide meals into individual portions using meal prep containers, which makes it easy to grab and go during busy weekdays. This also helps with portion control and ensures a balance of macronutrients in each meal.

USE TIME-SAVING TOOLS

Invest in kitchen appliances and tools that can make meal prep more efficient, such as a slow cooker, Instant Pot, or food processor.

KEEP IT SIMPLE

Focus on simple, flavorful recipes that can be prepared quickly and easily. As you become more comfortable with meal prepping, you can experiment with new recipes and techniques to keep your meals interesting and enjoyable.

PREPARE SNACKS

Pre-portion healthy, high-protein snacks like Greek yogurt with berries, sliced veggies with hummus, or mixed nuts. This makes it easy to grab a nutrient-dense snack when hunger strikes between meals.

PORTION CONTROL

UNDERSTAND SERVING SIZES

Familiarize yourself with appropriate serving sizes for different food groups. For example, a serving of protein should be about the size of your palm, a serving of grains should be about the size of your fist, and a serving of healthy fats should be about the size of your thumb.

USE SMALLER PLATES

Using smaller plates can make your portions appear larger, which may help you feel more satisfied with less food. This can be a simple yet effective way to encourage portion control.

MEASURE AND WEIGH FOOD

Using measuring cups, spoons, or a food scale can help you accurately determine portion sizes, especially when you're first getting started with portion control. Over time, you'll likely become more skilled at estimating appropriate portion sizes without needing to measure.

By incorporating these portion control strategies into your daily routine, you can support your Met Flex Diet goals, maintain a healthy weight, and improve your overall relationship with food.

PRE-PORTION MEALS

When meal prepping, divide your meals into individual portions using meal prep containers. This not only makes it easy to grab a meal on-the-go but also helps ensure that each meal has a balance of macronutrients and appropriate portion sizes.

SLOW DOWN AND BE MINDFUL

Eating slowly and mindfully can help you better recognize your body's hunger and fullness cues. This can prevent overeating and make it easier to control portion sizes.

HYDRATE BEFORE MEALS

Drinking a glass of water before a meal can help you feel fuller, which may lead to consuming smaller portions.

PRIORITIZE PROTEIN AND FIBER

Foods high in protein and fiber, such as lean meats, legumes, whole grains, and vegetables, can help you feel fuller for longer. By incorporating these foods into your meals, you may be less likely to overeat.

LISTEN TO YOUR BODY

Learn to recognize when you're genuinely hungry and when you're full. By honoring your body's hunger and fullness cues, you can develop a healthier relationship with food and practice better portion control.

DON'T DEPRIVE YOURSELF

Restricting yourself too much can often backfire, leading to overeating or binge eating. Allow yourself occasional treats in moderation to help prevent deprivation.

MINDFUL EATING

Mindful eating is a practice that involves being fully present and aware of your eating experience, paying attention to your body's hunger and fullness cues, and appreciating the flavors, textures, and sensations of your food.

ELIMINATE DISTRACTIONS

When eating, try to remove distractions like watching TV, scrolling through your phone, or working. Creating a distraction-free environment allows you to focus on your meal and fully appreciate the eating experience.

EAT SLOWLY

Take your time to chew and savor each bite. This not only helps improve digestion but also allows your body time to register fullness, preventing overeating.

PAY ATTENTION TO YOUR SENSES

Engage all your senses while eating. Notice the colors, textures, smells, and tastes of your food. This can make your meals more enjoyable and satisfying.

BE PRESENT

Focus on the experience of eating, including the flavors and textures of your food, the sensation of chewing, and the feeling of satisfaction as you nourish your body.

LISTEN TO YOUR BODY

Learn to recognize your body's hunger and fullness cues, and respond to them appropriately. Eat when you're genuinely hungry and stop when you're comfortably full.

PRACTICE GRATITUDE

Take a moment before each meal to express gratitude for the food you're about to eat. This can help you feel more connected to your food and foster a greater appreciation for the nourishment it provides.

PAUSE BETWEEN BITES

Set your utensils down between bites, allowing yourself a brief pause to fully savor your food and assess your hunger and fullness levels.

USE SMALLER PLATES AND UTENSILS

Using smaller plates can help control portion sizes, while using smaller utensils can encourage slower eating and increased mindfulness during meals.

BE COMPASSIONATE WITH YOURSELF

It's normal to have moments where you eat mindlessly or emotionally. Practice self-compassion and use these moments as opportunities to learn and grow in your mindful eating journey.

By incorporating mindful eating into your daily routine, you can develop a healthier relationship with food, better control your portions, and enhance your overall eating experience.

ADJUSTING THE PLAN FOR PERSONAL PREFERENCES

The Met Flex Diet is a flexible dietary approach that can be tailored to individual preferences, dietary restrictions, and lifestyle needs. Here are some tips for adjusting the plan to suit your unique requirements:

ACCOUNT FOR DIETARY RESTRICTIONS

Vegetarian or vegan: Replace animal-based protein sources with plant-based alternatives such as legumes, tofu, tempeh, seitan, and plant-based protein powders. Ensure adequate intake of essential nutrients like iron, vitamin B12, and omega-3 fatty acids through fortified foods or supplements, if necessary.

Gluten-free: Opt for gluten-free whole grains like quinoa, rice, millet, and certified gluten-free oats. Be mindful of hidden sources of gluten in processed foods and sauces.

Lactose intolerant: Choose lactose-free or low-lactose dairy products, such as lactose-free milk, yogurt, and cheese, or opt for plant-based milk and yogurt alternatives.

CONSIDER PERSONAL TASTE PREFERENCES

Experiment with different protein sources, whole grains, fruits, vegetables, and healthy fats to discover which foods you enjoy most.

Try out various herbs, spices, and flavorings to make your meals more interesting and appealing to your taste buds.

ADAPT TO YOUR ACTIVITY LEVELS

Adjust your carbohydrate intake based on your daily activity levels. On days with more intense workouts or physical activity, consider incorporating more carbohydrates into your meals, while on less active days, reduce your carbohydrate intake.

MODIFY MEAL TIMING AND FREQUENCY

While the Met Flex Diet generally recommends 3 main meals and 1-2 snacks per day, you can adjust this based on your personal preferences, work schedule, or lifestyle. Some individuals may prefer smaller, more frequent meals, while others may thrive on fewer, larger meals.

If you're interested in incorporating intermittent fasting, choose an eating window and fasting period that suits your lifestyle and individual needs.

CUSTOMIZE CARB CYCLING

The Met Flex Diet includes carb cycling to enhance metabolic flexibility. However, the specific number of higher-carb and lower-carb days can be adjusted based on your personal preferences, goals, and activity levels. Experiment with different carb cycling patterns to find the one that works best for you.

THE 4-WEEK
Met Flex Diet Plan

KICK-START METABOLIC FLEXIBILITY

Week 01

In the first week of the Met Flex Diet, the primary focus is on building a strong foundation for metabolic flexibility by gradually reducing processed foods and added sugars while increasing the intake of whole, nutrient-dense foods. Here's a breakdown of the key action steps and guidelines for Week 1:

ELIMINATE OR MINIMIZE PROCESSED FOODS AND ADDED SUGARS

Processed foods and added sugars can contribute to metabolic inflexibility and hinder your progress. Aim to remove or significantly reduce your intake of these foods, such as candy, soda, baked goods, and packaged snacks.

PRIORITIZE LEAN PROTEIN SOURCES

Protein is essential for maintaining and building muscle, as well as promoting satiety. Focus on including lean protein sources in your meals, such as chicken, turkey, fish, eggs, and plant-based options like beans, lentils, and tofu.

INCLUDE HEALTHY FATS

Healthy fats play an essential role in overall health and can help with satiety. Incorporate sources of healthy fats, such as avocados, nuts, seeds, olive oil, and fatty fish like salmon and mackerel.

INCORPORATE WHOLE GRAINS, FRUITS, AND VEGETABLES

Replace refined grains and processed carbohydrates with nutrient-dense, fiber-rich whole grains, fruits, and vegetables. Examples include brown rice, quinoa, barley, whole wheat pasta, leafy greens, cruciferous vegetables, berries, and citrus fruits.

DRINK AT LEAST 8 CUPS (64 OUNCES) OF WATER DAILY

Staying hydrated is crucial for overall health and can help with appetite regulation. Aim to consume at least 8 cups of water per day, and consider drinking more if you're physically active or live in a hot climate.

PLAN YOUR MEALS

Create a meal plan for the week that incorporates the Met Flex Diet principles, focusing on whole, nutrient-dense foods, lean proteins, complex carbohydrates, and healthy fats. This will help you stay organized and make it easier to stick to the plan.

INTRODUCE CARB CYCLING

Week 02

In the second week of the Met Flex Diet, you'll introduce carb cycling to enhance metabolic flexibility and optimize your body's ability to switch between burning carbohydrates and fats for fuel. Here's a breakdown of the key action steps and guidelines for Week 2:

DETERMINE YOUR CARB CYCLING PATTERN
Carb cycling involves alternating between higher-carb and lower-carb days throughout the week. A simple pattern to start with is two higher-carb days followed by five lower-carb days, but feel free to adjust this according to your personal preferences, goals, and activity levels.

MAINTAIN PROTEIN AND HEALTHY FAT INTAKE
Continue to prioritize lean protein sources and healthy fats in your meals, as these nutrients are essential for maintaining muscle mass, supporting overall health, and keeping you satisfied.

MONITOR YOUR ENERGY LEVELS AND PERFORMANCE
As you introduce carb cycling, pay attention to how your body responds in terms of energy levels, workout performance, and hunger signals. Make adjustments to your carb cycling pattern or carbohydrate intake as needed to support your personal needs and goals.

CALCULATE YOUR CARBOHYDRATE NEEDS
Higher-carb days: On these days, aim for approximately 45-50% of your total daily calories to come from carbohydrates. For example, if you consume 2,000 calories per day, you'll want to eat around 225-250 grams of carbohydrates on higher-carb days.

Lower-carb days: On these days, aim for approximately 25-30% of your total daily calories to come from carbohydrates. For example, if you consume 2,000 calories per day, you'll want to eat around 125-150 grams of carbohydrates on lower-carb days.

FOCUS ON NUTRIENT-DENSE CARBOHYDRATE SOURCES
Choose whole, unprocessed sources of carbohydrates, such as whole grains (e.g., brown rice, quinoa, whole wheat pasta), fruits, and starchy vegetables (e.g., sweet potatoes, squash, legumes). These foods provide essential nutrients and fiber, promoting overall health and satiety.

By incorporating carb cycling into your Met Flex Diet plan during Week 2, you'll begin to optimize your metabolic flexibility, teaching your body to efficiently switch between burning carbohydrates and fats for fuel.

BALANCE YOUR MACROS

Week 03

In the third week of the Met Flex Diet, you will focus on fine-tuning the balance of macronutrients in your meals—protein, carbohydrates, and fats—to support your personal goals, preferences, and activity levels. Here's a breakdown of the key action steps and guidelines for Week 3:

DETERMINE YOUR MACRONUTRIENT GOALS

Calculate your optimal macronutrient distribution based on your individual needs and goals. A general guideline is to aim for 40% carbohydrates, 30% protein, and 30% fats. However, you can adjust these percentages based on your specific preferences and requirements.

TRACK YOUR MACRONUTRIENT INTAKE

Use a food diary or a smartphone app to track your daily intake of protein, carbohydrates, and fats. Monitoring your macronutrient intake can help ensure you're meeting your goals and making any necessary adjustments.

PLAN BALANCED MEALS

Create meal plans that incorporate your macronutrient goals while focusing on whole, nutrient-dense foods. Each meal should include a source of lean protein, complex carbohydrates, healthy fats, and plenty of vegetables.

ADJUST FOR CARB CYCLING

Remember to take carb cycling into account when planning your meals and tracking your macros. On higher-carb days, increase your carbohydrate intake while slightly reducing fat intake. On lower-carb days, decrease your carbohydrate intake while moderately increasing your fat intake.

PAY ATTENTION TO YOUR BODY'S RESPONSE

Monitor your energy levels, workout performance, and overall well-being as you fine-tune your macronutrient balance. Adjust your macronutrient goals as needed to ensure you're feeling your best and making progress towards your health and fitness goals.

CONTINUE MINDFUL EATING AND HYDRATION PRACTICES

Maintain your focus on mindful eating, being aware of your hunger and fullness cues, and savoring the flavors and textures of your meals. Stay consistent with your hydration goals, aiming for at least 8 cups (64 ounces) of water per day.

By balancing your macronutrients and fine-tuning your meal plans in Week 3 of the Met Flex Diet, you'll further support metabolic flexibility and ensure that your diet is personalized to your unique needs, preferences, and goals, setting you up for long-term success.

MASTER MET FLEX EATING

Week 04

In the fourth week of the Met Flex Diet, you will focus on solidifying your new eating habits, making adjustments as needed, and planning for long-term success. Here's a breakdown of the key action steps and guidelines for Week 4:

REVIEW YOUR PROGRESS
Reflect on your progress over the past three weeks, considering any changes in energy levels, workout performance, weight, and overall well-being. Identify areas where you've been successful and areas where you may need to make adjustments.

REFINE YOUR MACRONUTRIENT BALANCE
Based on your observations and progress, make any necessary adjustments to your macronutrient goals and meal plans. This may involve tweaking your carbohydrate, protein, or fat intake to better support your unique needs and goals.

OPTIMIZE YOUR CARB CYCLING PATTERN
Evaluate your carb cycling pattern and make any necessary adjustments based on your personal preferences, activity levels, and progress. This may involve experimenting with different carb cycling patterns or adjusting the number of higher-carb and lower-carb days.

PLAN FOR LONG-TERM SUCCESS
Develop strategies for maintaining your Met Flex eating habits in the long term. This may include creating a collection of go-to recipes, developing meal prep routines, and establishing strategies for managing social events, travel, and other challenges.

EMPHASIZE MINDFUL EATING AND SELF-COMPASSION
Continue practicing mindful eating and cultivate self-compassion in your relationship with food. Recognize that setbacks are a normal part of the process and use them as opportunities to learn and grow.

STAY ACTIVE AND INCORPORATE EXERCISE
Regular physical activity is essential for overall health and can enhance metabolic flexibility. Develop a consistent exercise routine that includes both cardiovascular and resistance training to support your health and fitness goals.

By mastering Met Flex eating habits in Week 4 and planning for long-term success, you'll be well-equipped to maintain your newfound metabolic flexibility and continue reaping the benefits of this dietary approach. Remember that the journey doesn't end after four weeks; it's an ongoing process that requires consistent effort and adaptability.

Chapter 04
Breakfast
Recipes

15 Mouth-watering
Breakfast Recipes

TABLE OF CONTENTS

Greek Yogurt with Mixed Berries and Nuts

 Serving(s):
01

 Preparing:
10 mins

 Cooking:
N/A

Packed with protein, healthy fats, and antioxidants, this easy-to-make dish is perfect for the Met Flex Diet or anyone looking to enjoy a wholesome treat. It's also customizable, so feel free to mix and match your favorite berries and nuts.

Ingredients

1 cup non-fat plain Greek yogurt

1/2 cup mixed berries (strawberries, blueberries, raspberries, and blackberries)

1/4 cup mixed nuts (almonds, walnuts, and pecans)

1 tbsp honey or maple syrup (optional)

Instructions

1. Wash the mixed berries and pat dry with a clean towel.

2. In a serving bowl, add the Greek yogurt.

3. Top the yogurt with the mixed berries.

4. Sprinkle the mixed nuts over the berries.

5. Drizzle honey or maple syrup over the top, if desired.

6. Serve immediately, or refrigerate for up to 30 minutes to allow the flavors to meld.

Nutrients (per serving)

Calories: 380　　　Protein: 24g　　　Fat: 18g　　　Carbohydrates: 35g　　　Fiber: 6g　　　Sugar: 23g

Vegetable Omelette

 Serving(s):
01

 Preparing:
10 mins

 Cooking:
10 mins

Loaded with colorful veggies and protein-packed eggs, this dish is a great option for anyone following the Met Flex Diet or just looking for a nutritious, satisfying meal. Customize it with your favorite vegetables and seasonings for a personalized touch.

Ingredients

2 large eggs

1 tbsp olive oil or butter

1/4 cup diced bell pepper

1/4 cup diced onion

1/4 cup diced tomato

1/4 cup chopped spinach or kale

1/4 cup shredded cheese (optional, choose low-fat for a healthier option)

Salt and pepper, to taste

Fresh herbs, such as parsley or chives (optional)

Instructions

1. In a medium bowl, whisk the eggs until well beaten. Season with a pinch of salt and pepper, and set aside.
2. Heat the olive oil or butter in a non-stick skillet over medium heat.
3. Add the diced bell pepper and onion to the skillet and sauté for 3-4 minutes, or until the vegetables are softened and lightly browned.
4. Add the diced tomato and chopped spinach or kale to the skillet and cook for an additional 2 minutes, until the greens are wilted.
5. Pour the beaten eggs evenly over the vegetables in the skillet.
6. Cook the omelette for 2-3 minutes, lifting the edges gently with a spatula to allow the uncooked egg to flow underneath.
7. If using cheese, sprinkle it evenly over one half of the omelette.
8. Carefully fold the omelette in half, covering the cheese (if used) with the other half of the omelette.
9. Cook for an additional 1-2 minutes or until the eggs are fully set and the cheese has melted.
10. Slide the omelette onto a plate, garnish with fresh herbs if desired, and serve immediately.

Nutrients (per serving, without cheese)

Calories: 320	Protein: 16g	Fat: 24g	Carbohydrates: 9g	Fiber: 2g	Sugar: 5g

Cottage Cheese Pancakes

 Serving(s): 04

 Preparing: 10 mins

 Cooking: 10 mins

Cottage Cheese Pancakes are a protein-rich, healthy, and delicious alternative to traditional pancakes, perfect for those following the Met Flex Diet or anyone seeking a nutritious breakfast option.

Ingredients

1 cup cottage cheese (preferably low-fat or fat-free)

3/4 cup rolled oats

4 large eggs

1 tsp vanilla extract

1 tbsp honey or sweetener of your choice (optional)

1/4 tsp salt

1/2 tsp baking powder

Non-stick cooking spray or a small amount of butter for greasing the pan

Optional toppings: fresh fruit, Greek yogurt, nut butter, or maple syrup

Instructions

1. In a blender, combine the cottage cheese, rolled oats, eggs, vanilla extract, honey (or sweetener, if using), salt, and baking powder. Blend on high speed until smooth and well combined.

2. Preheat a non-stick skillet or griddle over medium heat and lightly grease it with non-stick cooking spray or a small amount of butter.

3. Pour 1/4 cup portions of the pancake batter onto the preheated skillet, spreading the batter out slightly with the back of a spoon or a spatula.

4. Cook the pancakes for 2-3 minutes, or until bubbles form on the surface and the edges appear set. Carefully flip the pancakes and cook for an additional 1-2 minutes, or until they are golden brown and cooked through.

5. Transfer the cooked pancakes to a plate and repeat with the remaining batter.

6. Serve the Cottage Cheese Pancakes warm with your choice of toppings, such as fresh fruit, Greek yogurt, nut butter, or maple syrup.

Nutrients (per serving, without cheese)

Calories: 180	Protein: 14g	Fat: 7g	Carbohydrates: 13g	Fiber: 1g	Sugar: 4g

Protein Smoothie

 Serving(s):
01

 Preparing:
05 mins

 Cooking:
N/A

A Protein Smoothie is a fantastic way to start your day or refuel after a workout. It's loaded with protein, vitamins, and minerals, making it an ideal choice for those following the Met Flex Diet or anyone looking for a nutrient-dense, delicious drink.

Ingredients

1 scoop (about 30g) protein powder (whey, plant-based, or your preferred type)

1 cup unsweetened almond milk, soy milk, or milk of choice

1/2 cup frozen mixed berries (strawberries, blueberries, raspberries)

1/2 banana

1/2 cup spinach or kale (optional)

1 tbsp chia seeds or flaxseeds (optional)

A few ice cubes (optional)

Instructions

1. In a blender, add the protein powder, almond milk, frozen mixed berries, banana, and spinach or kale (if using).

2. Blend on high speed for 30 seconds or until the mixture is smooth and creamy. If the smoothie is too thick, add a little more almond milk and blend again.

3. Add the chia seeds or flaxseeds (if using) and blend on low speed for a few seconds to incorporate them into the smoothie.

4. If desired, add ice cubes and blend again to reach your preferred thickness.

5. Pour the smoothie into a glass and enjoy immediately.

Nutrients (per serving, using whey protein and almond milk)

Calories: 300	Protein: 25g	Fat: 8g	Carbohydrates: 34g	Fiber: 8g	Sugar: 18g

Turkey and Spinach Scramble

 Serving(s): 01   *Preparing:* 10 mins   *Cooking:* 10 mins

This dish is packed with lean protein from the turkey and eggs, as well as essential vitamins and minerals from the spinach, making it an excellent choice for those following the Met Flex Diet or simply looking for a nutritious meal.

Ingredients

2 large eggs

1 tbsp olive oil or butter

1/4 cup diced onion

1/2 cup ground turkey (cooked)

1 cup fresh spinach, roughly chopped

Salt and pepper, to taste

Optional toppings: chopped fresh herbs (such as parsley, cilantro, or chives), hot sauce, or salsa

Instructions

1. In a medium bowl, whisk the eggs until well beaten. Season with a pinch of salt and pepper, and set aside.

2. Heat the olive oil or butter in a non-stick skillet over medium heat.

3. Add the diced onion to the skillet and sauté for 3-4 minutes, or until softened and lightly browned.

4. Add the cooked ground turkey to the skillet, stirring to combine with the onions.

5. Add the chopped spinach to the skillet, stirring until the spinach wilts slightly.

6. Pour the beaten eggs evenly over the turkey and spinach mixture in the skillet.

7. Cook the scramble, stirring gently, for 3-4 minutes or until the eggs are cooked through and no longer runny.

8. Season the scramble with additional salt and pepper, if desired.

9. Transfer the scramble to a plate, garnish with optional toppings, and serve immediately.

Nutrients (per serving)

Calories: 380   Protein: 33g   Fat: 22g   Carbohydrates: 10g   Fiber: 2g   Sugar: 4g

Avocado and Smoked Salmon

 Serving(s):
01

 Preparing:
10 mins

 Cooking:
N/A

Rich in healthy fats, protein, and essential nutrients, this dish is an excellent choice for those following the Met Flex Diet or anyone looking for a flavorful, nutrient-dense option.

Ingredients

1 ripe avocado, halved and pitted

4 oz smoked salmon, thinly sliced

1 tbsp lemon juice

Salt and pepper, to taste

Optional garnishes: capers, thinly sliced red onion, chopped fresh dill or chives

Instructions

1. Using a spoon, carefully scoop out the avocado halves from their skins, keeping them intact.

2. Place the avocado halves on a plate, cut side up.

3. Squeeze the lemon juice over the avocado halves, then season with a pinch of salt and pepper.

4. Drape the smoked salmon slices over the avocado halves, allowing the salmon to fold and curl naturally.

5. If desired, garnish the dish with capers, thinly sliced red onion, and chopped fresh dill or chives for added flavor and texture.

6. Serve immediately, or refrigerate for up to 30 minutes to allow the flavors to meld.

Nutrients (per serving)

Calories: 370	Protein: 22g	Fat: 28g	Carbohydrates: 10g	Fiber: 7g	Sugar: 1g

Keto Breakfast Muffins

 Serving(s):
12

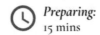 *Preparing:*
15 mins

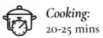 *Cooking:*
20-25 mins

Packed with protein, healthy fats, and essential nutrients, these muffins make a great grab-and-go breakfast or snack.
Customize the recipe with your favorite vegetables, meats, or cheeses for added variety and flavor.

Ingredients

6 large eggs

1/4 cup almond flour

1/2 cup grated cheddar cheese
(or cheese of choice)

1/2 cup cooked and crumbled
bacon or sausage (optional)

1/4 cup diced bell pepper

1/4 cup diced onion

1/4 cup chopped spinach or
kale

Salt and pepper, to taste

Cooking spray or muffin
liners

Instructions

1. Preheat your oven to 350°F (175°C). Grease a 12-cup muffin tin with cooking spray or line with muffin liners.
2. In a large bowl, whisk the eggs until well beaten.
3. Add the almond flour to the bowl and whisk until well combined with the eggs.
4. Stir in the grated cheese, cooked bacon or sausage (if using), diced bell pepper, diced onion, and chopped spinach or kale.
5. Season the mixture with salt and pepper, to taste.
6. Spoon the mixture evenly into the prepared muffin tin, filling each cup about 2/3 full.
7. Bake the muffins for 20-25 minutes, or until they are set in the center and lightly golden on top.
8. Remove the muffins from the oven and allow them to cool in the tin for 5 minutes before transferring them to a wire rack to cool completely.
9. Serve the muffins warm, or store them in an airtight container in the refrigerator for up to 4 days.

Nutrients (per muffin, assuming 12 muffins)

Calories: 110	Protein: 7g	Fat: 8g	Carbohydrates: 2g	Fiber: 1g	Sugar: 1g

Chia Seed Pudding

 Serving(s):
01

 Preparing:
10 mins

 Cooking:
N/A

Chia Seed Pudding is a healthy and delicious breakfast or dessert option that is perfect for those following the Met Flex Diet or anyone looking for a nutritious, fiber-rich treat.

Ingredients

1/4 cup chia seeds

1 cup unsweetened almond milk, coconut milk, or milk of choice

1 tbsp honey, maple syrup, or sweetener of choice (optional)

1/2 tsp vanilla extract

A pinch of salt

Optional toppings: fresh fruit (such as berries, sliced banana, or kiwi), nuts, seeds, or a dollop of Greek yogurt

Instructions

1. In a small bowl or jar, combine the chia seeds, almond milk, honey or sweetener (if using), vanilla extract, and a pinch of salt.

2. Stir the mixture well to ensure the chia seeds are evenly distributed throughout the liquid.

3. Cover the bowl or jar and refrigerate for at least 4 hours, or overnight, to allow the chia seeds to absorb the liquid and thicken the mixture into a pudding-like consistency. Stir the mixture occasionally during this time to prevent clumping.

4. After the chia seed pudding has thickened, give it a final stir and taste, adjusting the sweetness if desired.

5. Serve the chia seed pudding in a bowl or glass, topped with your choice of fresh fruit, nuts, seeds, or a dollop of Greek yogurt.

Nutrients (per serving, without optional sweetener or toppings)

Calories: 210	Protein: 7g	Fat: 14g	Carbohydrates: 16g	Fiber: 13g	Sugar: 1g

Almond Flour Pancakes

 Serving(s): 04   **Preparing:** 10 mins   **Cooking:** 10-15 mins

Almond Flour Pancakes are a delicious and nutritious alternative to traditional pancakes, perfect for those following the Met Flex Diet or anyone looking for a gluten-free, low-carb option.

Ingredients

1 1/2 cups almond flour

1/2 tsp baking powder

1/4 tsp salt

3 large eggs

1/4 cup unsweetened almond milk or milk of choice

1 tbsp honey or maple syrup (optional)

1 tsp vanilla extract

Butter or coconut oil, for greasing the pan

Optional toppings: fresh fruit, yogurt, nuts, or sugar-free syrup

Instructions

1. In a medium bowl, whisk together the almond flour, baking powder, and salt.
2. In a separate bowl, whisk together the eggs, almond milk, honey or maple syrup (if using), and vanilla extract.
3. Pour the wet ingredients into the dry ingredients, and mix until well combined and a batter forms.
4. Preheat a non-stick skillet or griddle over medium-low heat. Lightly grease the skillet with butter or coconut oil.
5. Pour 1/4 cup of batter onto the skillet for each pancake, spreading the batter out slightly to form a round pancake shape.
6. Cook the pancakes for 2-3 minutes, or until the edges start to set and the bottom is lightly golden brown. Carefully flip the pancakes and cook for another 2-3 minutes, or until the pancakes are cooked through and golden brown on both sides.
7. Transfer the cooked pancakes to a plate, and continue with the remaining batter, greasing the skillet as needed.
8. Serve the almond flour pancakes warm, topped with your choice of fresh fruit, yogurt, nuts, or sugar-free syrup.

Nutrients (per serving, without optional sweetener or toppings)

| Calories: 310 | Protein: 13g | Fat: 25g | Carbohydrates: 12g | Fiber: 5g | Sugar: 3g |

Cauliflower Hash Browns

 Serving(s):
04

 Preparing:
15 mins

 *Cooking:*
10-15 mins

Made with cauliflower instead of potatoes, these hash browns are packed with vitamins and minerals, making them a healthy and satisfying choice for breakfast or brunch. Customize the recipe with your favorite herbs and seasonings for added flavor.

Ingredients

1 medium head cauliflower, riced (about 4 cups)

1/4 cup grated Parmesan cheese

1/4 cup almond flour or coconut flour

1 large egg

1/2 tsp garlic powder

1/2 tsp onion powder

Salt and pepper, to taste

2-3 tbsps olive oil, for frying

Instructions

1. To rice the cauliflower, either grate it using the large holes of a box grater or pulse florets in a food processor until it resembles rice.
2. Place the riced cauliflower in a microwave-safe bowl, cover with a microwave-safe plate or plastic wrap, and microwave on high for 3-4 minutes to soften.
3. Allow the cauliflower to cool slightly, then transfer it to a clean kitchen towel or cheesecloth. Squeeze out as much liquid as possible from the cauliflower.
4. In a large bowl, combine the squeezed cauliflower, Parmesan cheese, almond or coconut flour, egg, garlic powder, onion powder, salt, and pepper. Mix well to form a dough-like consistency.
5. Preheat the olive oil in a non-stick skillet over medium heat.
6. Scoop 1/4 cup of the cauliflower mixture onto the skillet for each hash brown, flattening it out slightly to form a patty shape.
7. Fry the hash browns for 4-5 minutes on each side, or until they are golden brown and crispy. Be careful when flipping to avoid breaking the hash browns.
8. Transfer the cooked hash browns to a paper towel-lined plate to drain any excess oil, then serve immediately.

Nutrients (per serving)

Calories: 190	Protein: 8g	Fat: 14g	Carbohydrates: 10g	Fiber: 4g	Sugar: 3g

Overnight Oats

 Serving(s):
01

 Preparing:
15 mins

 Cooking:
N/A

Perfect for those following the Met Flex Diet or anyone looking for a nutritious, fiber-rich meal, overnight oats are prepared the night before and ready to eat in the morning.

Ingredients

1/2 cup rolled oats

1/2 cup unsweetened almond milk, coconut milk, or milk of choice

1/2 cup Greek yogurt or yogurt of choice

1 tbsp chia seeds

1 tbsp honey, maple syrup, or sweetener of choice (optional)

1/2 tsp vanilla extract

A pinch of salt

Optional toppings: fresh fruit (such as berries, sliced banana, or diced apple), nuts, seeds, or a sprinkle of cinnamon

Instructions

1. In a mason jar or airtight container, combine the rolled oats, almond milk, Greek yogurt, chia seeds, honey or sweetener (if using), vanilla extract, and a pinch of salt.

2. Stir the mixture well to ensure the oats and chia seeds are evenly distributed throughout the liquid.

3. Cover the jar or container and refrigerate for at least 6 hours, or overnight, to allow the oats and chia seeds to absorb the liquid and soften.

4. In the morning, give the overnight oats a good stir, then taste and adjust the sweetness if desired.

5. Serve the overnight oats cold, topped with your choice of fresh fruit, nuts, seeds, or a sprinkle of cinnamon.

Nutrients (per serving, without optional sweetener or toppings)

| Calories: 290 | Protein: 15g | Fat: 9g | Carbohydrates: 36g | Fiber: 7g | Sugar: 5g |

Whole Grain Toast with Avocado and Poached Egg

 Serving(s): 01

 Preparing: 10 mins

 Cooking: 05-10 mins

Whole Grain Toast with Avocado and Poached Egg is a delicious and nutritious breakfast option, perfect for those following the Met Flex Diet or anyone looking for a well-rounded, protein-rich meal.

Ingredients

2 slices whole grain bread

1 ripe avocado

2 large eggs

1 tbsp white vinegar (optional, for poaching eggs)

Salt and pepper, to taste

Optional toppings: red pepper flakes, chopped fresh herbs (such as parsley or cilantro), or a drizzle of hot sauce

Instructions

1. Toast the whole grain bread to your desired level of crispiness.
2. Cut the avocado in half, remove the pit, and scoop out the flesh. Use a fork to mash the avocado in a small bowl, seasoning with salt and pepper to taste.
3. To poach the eggs, fill a saucepan with water and bring it to a gentle simmer. Add the white vinegar (if using) to help the egg whites set more quickly.
4. Crack one egg into a small bowl or ramekin, then carefully slide it into the simmering water. Repeat with the second egg. Cook the eggs for 3-4 minutes for a runny yolk, or 4-5 minutes for a firmer yolk.
5. Use a slotted spoon to carefully remove the poached eggs from the water and place them on a paper towel-lined plate to drain any excess water.
6. Spread the mashed avocado evenly onto the toasted whole grain bread slices. Top each slice with a poached egg.
7. Season the eggs with salt and pepper, to taste, and garnish with optional toppings such as red pepper flakes, fresh herbs, or a drizzle of hot sauce.

Nutrients (per serving)

Calories: 480   Protein: 20g   Fat: 30g   Carbohydrates: 38g   Fiber: 11g   Sugar: 5g

Quinoa and Veggie Breakfast Bowl

 Serving(s): 01

 Preparing: 10 mins

 Cooking: 20-25 mins

Combining the protein and fiber of quinoa with a variety of vegetables and seasonings, this dish is a colorful and delicious choice for breakfast or brunch. Customize the recipe with your favorite veggies and seasonings for added variety and flavor.

Ingredients

1/2 cup uncooked quinoa

1 cup water or vegetable broth

1 tbsp olive oil

1/2 cup diced bell pepper (any color)

1/2 cup diced zucchini

1/4 cup diced red onion

1/4 cup cherry tomatoes, halved

1/4 cup chopped kale or spinach

Salt and pepper, to taste

Optional toppings: chopped fresh herbs (such as parsley or cilantro), sliced avocado, or a fried or poached egg

Instructions

1. Rinse the quinoa under cold water to remove any bitterness. In a small saucepan, combine the quinoa and water or vegetable broth. Bring to a boil, then reduce the heat, cover, and simmer for 15-20 minutes, or until the quinoa is cooked and the liquid has been absorbed. Fluff the quinoa with a fork and set aside.

2. In a large skillet, heat the olive oil over medium heat. Add the diced bell pepper, zucchini, and red onion. Cook, stirring occasionally, for 5-7 minutes, or until the vegetables are tender and lightly browned.

3. Add the cherry tomatoes and chopped kale or spinach to the skillet. Cook for an additional 2-3 minutes, or until the kale or spinach has wilted and the tomatoes are slightly softened.

4. Stir the cooked quinoa into the vegetable mixture, seasoning with salt and pepper to taste.

5. Transfer the quinoa and veggie mixture to a bowl, and top with optional toppings such as fresh herbs, sliced avocado, or a fried or poached egg.

Nutrients (per serving, without optional toppings)

| Calories: 420 | Protein: 14g | Fat: 14g | Carbohydrates: 60g | Fiber: 8g | Sugar: 5g |

Veggie and Cheese Breakfast Burrito

 Serving(s): 02

 Preparing: 10 mins

 Cooking: 15 mins

Veggie and Cheese Breakfast Burrito is a delicious and satisfying breakfast option, perfect for those following the Met Flex Diet or anyone looking for a protein-packed, veggie-filled meal.

Ingredients

1 tbsp olive oil

1/2 cup diced bell pepper (any color)

1/2 cup diced onion

1/2 cup diced zucchini or summer squash

1/2 cup chopped spinach or kale

4 large eggs

Salt and pepper, to taste

2 whole grain or low-carb tortillas

1/2 cup shredded cheese (such as cheddar, Monterey Jack, or pepper jack)

Optional toppings: salsa, hot sauce, avocado slices, or sour cream

Instructions

1. In a large skillet, heat the olive oil over medium heat. Add the diced bell pepper, onion, and zucchini. Cook, stirring occasionally, for 5-7 minutes, or until the vegetables are tender and lightly browned.
2. Add the chopped spinach or kale to the skillet and cook for an additional 1-2 minutes, or until wilted.
3. In a bowl, whisk the eggs, salt, and pepper together. Pour the egg mixture over the vegetables in the skillet, and cook, stirring occasionally, until the eggs are fully cooked and scrambled.
4. Warm the tortillas in the microwave for 10-15 seconds, or until they are pliable.
5. Divide the veggie and egg mixture evenly between the two tortillas, placing the mixture in the center of each tortilla. Sprinkle each tortilla with 1/4 cup of shredded cheese.
6. Fold in the sides of each tortilla, and then roll them up tightly to form a burrito.
7. Optional: For a crispy finish, heat a non-stick skillet over medium heat, and cook the burritos seam-side down for 2-3 minutes, or until lightly browned. Flip and cook for an additional 2-3 minutes.
8. Serve the breakfast burritos with optional toppings such as salsa, hot sauce, avocado slices, or sour cream.

Nutrients (per serving, without optional toppings)

Calories: 470   Protein: 28g   Fat: 29g   Carbohydrates: 20g   Fiber: 6g   Sugar: 5g

Peanut Butter and Banana Smoothie

 Serving(s):
01

 Preparing:
5 mins

 Cooking:
N/A

A Peanut Butter and Banana Smoothie is a creamy, delicious, and satisfying treat that is perfect for those following the Met Flex Diet or anyone seeking a healthy and protein-packed snack or breakfast option.

Ingredients

1 medium ripe banana, peeled and frozen

1 cup unsweetened almond milk (or milk of your choice)

1/2 cup plain Greek yogurt (or yogurt of your choice)

2 tbsps natural peanut butter (or nut butter of your choice)

1 tbsp honey or sweetener of your choice (optional)

1/2 tsp vanilla extract

A handful of ice cubes (optional)

Instructions

1. In a blender, combine the frozen banana, unsweetened almond milk (or milk of your choice), Greek yogurt (or yogurt of your choice), natural peanut butter, honey (or sweetener, if using), and vanilla extract.

2. Blend the ingredients on high speed until smooth and creamy, adding a handful of ice cubes if you prefer a thicker consistency.

3. Taste the smoothie and adjust the sweetness or flavorings as desired.

4. Pour the smoothie into a glass and serve immediately.

Nutrients (per serving, without sweetener)

| Calories: 380 | Protein: 18g | Fat: 19g | Carbohydrates: 40g | Fiber: 5g | Sugar: 24g |

Chapter 05

Lunch

Recipes

*15 Mouth-watering
Lunch Recipes*

TABLE OF CONTENTS

Grilled Chicken Salad

 Serving(s): 01

 Preparing: 10 mins

 Cooking: 10-15 mins

Nutrients
(per serving)

Calories: 330	Carbohydrates: 12g
Protein: 42g	Fiber: 3g
Fat: 14g	Sugar: 5g

Grilled Chicken Salad is a delicious and nutritious lunch or dinner option, perfect for those following the Met Flex Diet or anyone looking for a protein-packed, low-carb meal. Combining tender grilled chicken, fresh vegetables, and a light dressing, this dish is full of flavor and nutrients, making it a great choice for a satisfying and healthy meal.

Ingredients

1 boneless, skinless chicken breast (about 6 ounces)
Salt and pepper, to taste
Olive oil, for grilling
4 cups mixed greens (such as lettuce, spinach, or arugula)
1/2 cup cherry tomatoes, halved
1/4 cup diced cucumber
1/4 cup diced bell pepper (any color)
1/4 cup sliced red onion
1/4 cup crumbled feta cheese or goat cheese (optional)
Optional toppings: sliced avocado, toasted nuts or seeds, or croutons
Dressing: your choice of vinaigrette, low-fat ranch, or another low-calorie dressing

Instructions

1. Preheat your grill or grill pan to medium-high heat. Season the chicken breast with salt and pepper and lightly brush with olive oil.

2. Grill the chicken breast for 5-7 minutes per side, or until the internal temperature reaches 165°F (74°C) and the chicken is no longer pink in the center. Remove the chicken from the grill and let it rest for a few minutes before slicing.

3. In a large salad bowl, combine the mixed greens, cherry tomatoes, cucumber, bell pepper, and red onion. Toss the salad ingredients together to mix them evenly.

4. Top the salad with the sliced grilled chicken, crumbled cheese (if using), and any additional optional toppings.

5. Drizzle your choice of dressing over the salad, or serve the dressing on the side for individual preference.

Turkey and Quinoa Stuffed Peppers

 Serving(s): 04

 Preparing: 20 mins

 Cooking: 45-60 mins

Nutrients
(per serving)

Calories: 410	Carbohydrates: 32g
Protein: 35g	Fiber: 6g
Fat: 17g	Sugar: 9g

Turkey and Quinoa Stuffed Peppers are a delicious and nutritious meal option, perfect for those following the Met Flex Diet or anyone looking for a protein-packed, fiber-rich dish. Combining lean ground turkey, quinoa, and a variety of vegetables, this dish is full of flavor and nutrients, making it a great choice for a satisfying and healthy meal.

Ingredients

4 large bell peppers (any color), halved and seeded

1/2 cup uncooked quinoa

1 cup water or vegetable broth

1 tbsp olive oil

1 pound lean ground turkey

1/2 cup diced onion

2 cloves garlic, minced

1/2 cup diced zucchini

1/2 cup diced tomatoes

1/2 cup tomato sauce

1 tsp dried oregano

Salt and pepper, to taste

1 cup shredded cheese (such as cheddar, Monterey Jack, or mozzarella)

Optional toppings: chopped fresh herbs (such as parsley or cilantro), sour cream, or avocado slices

Instructions

1. Preheat your oven to 350°F (175°C). Arrange the halved bell peppers in a baking dish, cut side up.
2. Rinse the quinoa under cold water to remove any bitterness. In a small saucepan, combine the quinoa and water or vegetable broth. Bring to a boil, then reduce the heat, cover, and simmer for 15-20 minutes, or until the quinoa is cooked and the liquid has been absorbed. Fluff the quinoa with a fork and set aside.
3. In a large skillet, heat the olive oil over medium heat. Add the ground turkey, onion, and garlic, and cook until the turkey is browned and the onion is softened, about 5-7 minutes. Drain any excess fat from the skillet.
4. Add the diced zucchini, diced tomatoes, tomato sauce, oregano, salt, and pepper to the skillet. Cook for an additional 5 minutes, or until the vegetables are tender.
5. Stir the cooked quinoa into the turkey and vegetable mixture until well combined.
6. Spoon the turkey and quinoa mixture into the bell pepper halves, filling them evenly. Top each stuffed pepper with a portion of shredded cheese.
7. Cover the baking dish with aluminum foil and bake for 30 minutes. Remove the foil and bake for an additional 10-15 minutes, or until the peppers are tender and the cheese is melted and bubbly.
8. Serve the Turkey and Quinoa Stuffed Peppers with optional toppings such as fresh herbs, sour cream, or avocado slices.

Tofu Stir-Fry

 Serving(s): 04   *Preparing:* 15 mins   *Cooking:* 15-20 mins

Nutrients
(per serving, without optional toppings and side)

Calories: 320	Carbohydrates: 24g
Protein: 16g	Fiber: 4g
Fat: 18g	Sugar: 10g

Tofu Stir-Fry is a delicious and nutritious meal option, perfect for those following the Met Flex Diet or anyone looking for a protein-packed, plant-based dish. Combining firm tofu, a variety of vegetables, and a flavorful sauce, this dish is full of taste and nutrients, making it a great choice for a satisfying and healthy meal.

Ingredients

1 (14-ounce) block firm tofu, drained and pressed to remove excess water

1 tbsp cornstarch

3 tbsps vegetable oil, divided

1/2 cup diced bell pepper (any color)

1/2 cup diced onion

1/2 cup sliced carrots

1/2 cup sliced zucchini

1/2 cup broccoli florets

2 cloves garlic, minced

1/4 cup low-sodium soy sauce or tamari

1 tbsp rice vinegar

1 tbsp honey or maple syrup

1 tsp sriracha or chili-garlic sauce (optional, for heat)

Optional toppings: sesame seeds, chopped green onions, or chopped fresh cilantro

Optional side: cooked brown rice, quinoa, or cauliflower rice

Instructions

1. Cut the pressed tofu into 1-inch cubes and toss with cornstarch in a bowl until evenly coated.
2. In a large skillet or wok, heat 2 tbsps of vegetable oil over medium-high heat. Add the tofu cubes and cook, turning occasionally, until they are golden and crispy on all sides, about 5-7 minutes. Transfer the cooked tofu to a plate and set aside.
3. In the same skillet, heat the remaining 1 tbsp of vegetable oil over medium-high heat. Add the bell pepper, onion, carrots, zucchini, and broccoli florets. Cook, stirring frequently, for 5-7 minutes, or until the vegetables are tender and lightly browned.
4. Add the minced garlic to the skillet and cook for an additional 1 minute, or until fragrant.
5. In a small bowl, whisk together the soy sauce or tamari, rice vinegar, honey or maple syrup, and sriracha or chili-garlic sauce (if using).
6. Add the cooked tofu back to the skillet with the vegetables. Pour the sauce over the tofu and vegetables, and stir to coat everything evenly. Cook for an additional 2-3 minutes, or until the sauce has slightly thickened.
7. Remove the skillet from the heat and top the tofu stir-fry with optional toppings such as sesame seeds, chopped green onions, or chopped fresh cilantro.
8. Serve the Tofu Stir-Fry on its own or with an optional side of cooked brown rice, quinoa, or cauliflower rice.

Lentil Soup with Greens

 Serving(s): 04

 Preparing: 10 mins

 Cooking: 45-60 mins

Nutrients
(per serving, without optional toppings)

Calories: 280	Carbohydrates: 47g
Protein: 16g	Fiber: 19g
Fat: 4g	Sugar: 9g

Lentil Soup with Greens is a hearty and nutritious meal option, perfect for those following the Met Flex Diet or anyone looking for a protein-packed, plant-based dish. Combining lentils, a variety of vegetables, and leafy greens, this soup is full of flavor, fiber, and nutrients, making it a great choice for a satisfying and healthy meal.

Ingredients

1 cup dried green or brown lentils, rinsed and drained
1 tbsp olive oil
1 medium onion, diced
2 cloves garlic, minced
2 medium carrots, diced
2 celery stalks, diced
1 (14.5-ounce) can diced tomatoes
6 cups vegetable broth
1 tsp dried thyme
Salt and pepper, to taste
4 cups chopped leafy greens (such as kale, spinach, or Swiss chard)
Optional toppings: grated Parmesan cheese, a dollop of Greek yogurt, or chopped fresh parsley

Instructions

1. In a large pot, heat the olive oil over medium heat. Add the diced onion, garlic, carrots, and celery, and cook, stirring occasionally, for 5-7 minutes, or until the vegetables are softened and lightly browned.

2. Add the rinsed and drained lentils, diced tomatoes (with their juice), vegetable broth, dried thyme, salt, and pepper to the pot. Stir to combine.

3. Bring the soup to a boil, then reduce the heat and let it simmer, uncovered, for 30-40 minutes, or until the lentils are tender.

4. Stir in the chopped leafy greens, and cook for an additional 5-10 minutes, or until the greens are wilted and tender.

5. Taste the soup and adjust the seasoning with salt and pepper if necessary.

6. Serve the Lentil Soup with Greens hot, and top with optional toppings such as grated Parmesan cheese, a dollop of Greek yogurt, or chopped fresh parsley.

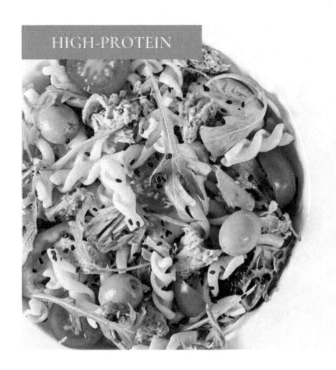

Tuna and White Bean Salad

 Serving(s): 04 **Preparing:** 15 mins **Cooking:** 15-120 mins

Nutrients
(per serving, without optional toppings)

Calories: 340   Carbohydrates: 35g

Protein: 25g   Fiber: 10g

Fat: 12g   Sugar: 4g

Tuna and White Bean Salad is a refreshing and nutritious meal option, perfect for those following the Met Flex Diet or anyone looking for a protein-packed, fiber-rich dish. Combining canned tuna, white beans, and a variety of vegetables, this salad is full of flavor and nutrients, making it a great choice for a satisfying and healthy meal.

Ingredients

1 (5-ounce) can tuna in water, drained and flaked

1 (15-ounce) can white beans (such as cannellini or Great Northern), rinsed and drained

1/2 cup diced red bell pepper

1/2 cup diced cucumber

1/4 cup finely chopped red onion

1/4 cup chopped fresh parsley

2 tbsps capers, drained (optional)

3 tbsps lemon juice

2 tbsps olive oil

Salt and pepper, to taste

Optional toppings: crumbled feta cheese or sliced avocado

Instructions

1. In a large bowl, combine the drained and flaked tuna, rinsed and drained white beans, diced red bell pepper, diced cucumber, chopped red onion, chopped fresh parsley, and capers (if using).

2. In a small bowl, whisk together the lemon juice and olive oil until well combined. Season the dressing with salt and pepper, to taste.

3. Pour the dressing over the tuna and white bean mixture and toss gently to coat all the ingredients evenly.

4. Allow the salad to sit for at least 15 minutes to allow the flavors to meld, or cover and refrigerate for up to 2 hours to serve chilled.

5. Serve the Tuna and White Bean Salad on its own or with optional toppings such as crumbled feta cheese or sliced avocado.

Greek Salad with Grilled Chicken

 Serving(s): 04   **Preparing:** 20 mins   **Cooking:** 10-15 mins

Nutrients
(per serving)

Calories: 460	Carbohydrates: 14g
Protein: 30g	Fiber: 3g
Fat: 32g	Sugar: 6g

Greek Salad with Grilled Chicken is a delicious and nutritious meal option, perfect for those following the Met Flex Diet or anyone looking for a protein-packed, low-carb dish. Combining fresh vegetables, flavorful feta cheese, and perfectly grilled chicken, this salad is full of taste and nutrients, making it a great choice for a satisfying and healthy meal.

Ingredients

For the Grilled Chicken:
2 boneless, skinless chicken breasts
2 tbsps olive oil
1 tbsp lemon juice
1 tsp dried oregano
Salt and pepper, to taste

For the Greek Salad:
4 cups chopped romaine lettuce
1 cup halved cherry tomatoes
1 cup diced cucumber
1/2 cup thinly sliced red onion
1/2 cup pitted Kalamata olives
1/2 cup crumbled feta cheese

For the Dressing:
1/4 cup olive oil
2 tbsps red wine vinegar
1 tbsp lemon juice
1 clove garlic, minced
1/2 tsp dried oregano
Salt and pepper, to taste

Instructions

For the Grilled Chicken:

1. In a small bowl, whisk together the olive oil, lemon juice, dried oregano, salt, and pepper. Place the chicken breasts in a shallow dish or resealable plastic bag and pour the marinade over them. Ensure the chicken is fully coated, then cover and refrigerate for at least 30 minutes, or up to 2 hours.

2. Preheat a grill or grill pan to medium-high heat. Remove the chicken breasts from the marinade and grill for 5-7 minutes per side, or until cooked through and the internal temperature reaches 165°F (74°C). Let the chicken rest for a few minutes before slicing.

For the Greek Salad:

1. In a large bowl, combine the chopped romaine lettuce, cherry tomatoes, diced cucumber, sliced red onion, Kalamata olives, and crumbled feta cheese.

For the Dressing:

1. In a small bowl or jar, whisk together the olive oil, red wine vinegar, lemon juice, minced garlic, dried oregano, salt, and pepper until well combined.

To Assemble:

1. Divide the Greek salad among four plates or bowls. Top each salad with sliced grilled chicken and drizzle with the dressing. Serve immediately.

Cauliflower Fried Rice with Shrimp

 Serving(s): 04

 Preparing: 15 mins

 Cooking: 15-20 mins

Nutrients
(per serving, without optional toppings)

Calories: 270	Carbohydrates: 17g
Protein: 22g	Fiber: 5g
Fat: 12g	Sugar: 5g

Cauliflower Fried Rice with Shrimp is a flavorful and nutritious meal option, perfect for those following the Met Flex Diet or anyone looking for a low-carb, protein-packed dish. Combining cauliflower rice, a variety of vegetables, and succulent shrimp, this dish is full of taste and nutrients, making it a great choice for a satisfying and healthy meal.

Ingredients

1 medium head of cauliflower, chopped into florets

1 tbsp vegetable oil, divided

1/2 cup diced onion

1/2 cup diced bell pepper (any color)

1/2 cup frozen peas and carrots, thawed

2 cloves garlic, minced

8 ounces raw shrimp, peeled and deveined

2 large eggs, beaten

3 tbsps low-sodium soy sauce or tamari

1 tbsp sesame oil

Salt and pepper, to taste

Optional toppings: chopped green onions or sesame seeds

Instructions

1. Place the cauliflower florets in a food processor and pulse until they resemble rice grains. You should have about 4 cups of cauliflower rice. Set aside.

2. In a large skillet or wok, heat 1/2 tbsp of vegetable oil over medium-high heat. Add the diced onion, bell pepper, and thawed peas and carrots. Cook, stirring frequently, for 5-7 minutes, or until the vegetables are tender and lightly browned.

3. Add the minced garlic to the skillet and cook for an additional 1 minute, or until fragrant.

4. Push the vegetables to one side of the skillet and add the remaining 1/2 tablespoon of vegetable oil to the empty side. Add the shrimp to the skillet and cook for 2-3 minutes per side, or until they are pink and cooked through. Remove the shrimp from the skillet and set aside.

5. Push the vegetables to one side of the skillet again and pour the beaten eggs into the empty side. Scramble the eggs until they are fully cooked, then mix them with the vegetables.

6. Add the cauliflower rice, cooked shrimp, soy sauce or tamari, and sesame oil to the skillet. Stir well to combine and cook for an additional 2-3 minutes, or until the cauliflower rice is tender and heated through.

7. Season the cauliflower fried rice with salt and pepper, to taste.

8. Serve the Cauliflower Fried Rice with Shrimp hot, and garnish with optional toppings such as chopped green onions or sesame seeds.

Zucchini Noodle Caprese Salad

 Serving(s): 04

 Preparing: 15 mins

 Cooking: 10-120 mins

Nutrients
(per serving, without optional toppings)

Calories: 270	Carbohydrates: 9g
Protein: 10g	Fiber: 2g
Fat: 22g	Sugar: 6g

Zucchini Noodle Caprese Salad is a light and nutritious meal option, perfect for those following the Met Flex Diet or anyone looking for a low-carb, protein-rich dish. Combining spiralized zucchini noodles, fresh mozzarella, cherry tomatoes, and fragrant basil, this salad is full of taste and nutrients, making it a great choice for a satisfying and healthy meal.

Ingredients

2 medium zucchini, ends trimmed

1 cup halved cherry tomatoes

1 cup fresh mozzarella balls (bocconcini) or cubed fresh mozzarella

1/2 cup fresh basil leaves, torn or chopped

1/4 cup extra-virgin olive oil

2 tbsps balsamic vinegar

Salt and pepper, to taste

Optional toppings: balsamic glaze or crushed red pepper flakes

Instructions

1. Using a spiralizer or a julienne peeler, create zucchini noodles (zoodles) from the zucchini. If desired, trim the zoodles to shorter, more manageable lengths. Place the zoodles in a large bowl.

2. Add the halved cherry tomatoes, fresh mozzarella balls or cubes, and fresh basil leaves to the bowl with the zucchini noodles.

3. In a small bowl, whisk together the extra-virgin olive oil and balsamic vinegar until well combined. Season the dressing with salt and pepper, to taste.

4. Pour the dressing over the zucchini noodle mixture and toss gently to coat all the ingredients evenly.

5. Allow the salad to sit for at least 10 minutes for the flavors to meld, or cover and refrigerate for up to 2 hours to serve chilled.

6. Serve the Zucchini Noodle Caprese Salad on its own or with optional toppings such as a drizzle of balsamic glaze or a sprinkle of crushed red pepper flakes.

Chicken Lettuce Wraps

 Serving(s): 04   **Preparing:** 15 mins   **Cooking:** 15-20 mins

Nutrients
(per serving, without optional toppings)

Calories: 280	Carbohydrates: 14g
Protein: 22g	Fiber: 2g
Fat: 15g	Sugar: 7g

Chicken Lettuce Wraps are a tasty and nutritious meal option, perfect for those following the Met Flex Diet or anyone looking for a low-carb, protein-packed dish. Combining sautéed ground chicken, flavorful Asian-inspired sauce, and crisp lettuce leaves, these wraps are full of taste and nutrients, making them a great choice for a satisfying and healthy meal.

Ingredients

1 pound ground chicken
1 tbsp vegetable oil
1/2 cup diced onion
1/2 cup diced bell pepper (any color)
2 cloves garlic, minced
1/4 cup hoisin sauce
2 tbsps low-sodium soy sauce or tamari
1 tbsp rice vinegar
1 tsp Sriracha or other hot sauce (optional, to taste)
1/2 cup chopped green onions
Salt and pepper, to taste
1 head of butter lettuce or iceberg lettuce, leaves separated and rinsed
Optional toppings: chopped peanuts, fresh cilantro, or sesame seeds

Instructions

1. In a large skillet, heat the vegetable oil over medium-high heat. Add the ground chicken and cook, breaking it apart with a spatula, until fully cooked and no longer pink, about 5-7 minutes. Remove the cooked chicken from the skillet and set aside.

2. In the same skillet, add the diced onion and bell pepper. Cook, stirring frequently, for 5-7 minutes, or until the vegetables are tender and lightly browned.

3. Add the minced garlic to the skillet and cook for an additional 1 minute, or until fragrant.

4. Return the cooked ground chicken to the skillet with the vegetables. Stir in the hoisin sauce, soy sauce or tamari, rice vinegar, and Sriracha (if using). Cook for 2-3 minutes, or until the sauce thickens and coats the chicken and vegetables.

5. Remove the skillet from heat and stir in the chopped green onions. Season the chicken mixture with salt and pepper, to taste.

6. To serve, spoon the chicken mixture onto the lettuce leaves, then garnish with optional toppings such as chopped peanuts, fresh cilantro, or sesame seeds.

Cobb Salad

 Serving(s): 04

 Preparing: 20 mins

 Cooking: N/A

Nutrients
(per serving, without dressing)

Calories: 525	Carbohydrates: 15g
Protein: 40g	Fiber: 6g
Fat: 33g	Sugar: 5g

Cobb Salad is a classic and nutritious meal option, perfect for those following the Met Flex Diet or anyone looking for a low-carb, protein-packed dish. With a mix of fresh greens, grilled chicken, crispy bacon, avocado, and more, this salad is full of flavor and nutrients, making it a great choice for a satisfying and healthy meal.

Ingredients

6 cups mixed salad greens (such as romaine, iceberg, or spinach)
1 pound grilled chicken breast, sliced or diced
4 hard-boiled eggs, peeled and quartered
6 slices cooked bacon, crumbled
1 medium avocado, pitted, peeled, and diced
1 cup halved cherry tomatoes
1/2 cup crumbled blue cheese (or feta cheese, if preferred)
1/4 cup chopped green onions
Salt and pepper, to taste
Your choice of salad dressing (such as ranch, blue cheese, or vinaigrette)

Instructions

1. In a large serving platter or individual salad plates, arrange the mixed salad greens as the base.

2. Arrange the grilled chicken, hard-boiled eggs, crumbled bacon, diced avocado, cherry tomatoes, crumbled blue cheese, and chopped green onions in rows or sections on top of the salad greens.

3. Season the salad with salt and pepper, to taste.

4. Serve the Cobb Salad with your choice of salad dressing on the side.

Veggie-Packed Whole Wheat Pita Sandwich

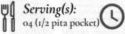 *Serving(s):* 04 (1/2 pita pocket)   *Preparing:* 15 mins   *Cooking:* N/A

Nutrients
(per serving, without optional protein)

Calories: 350	Carbohydrates: 47g
Protein: 12g	Fiber: 10g
Fat: 15g	Sugar: 6g

Cobb Salad is a classic and nutritious meal option, perfect for those following the Met Flex Diet or anyone looking for a low-carb, protein-packed dish. With a mix of fresh greens, grilled chicken, crispy bacon, avocado, and more, this salad is full of flavor and nutrients, making it a great choice for a satisfying and healthy meal.

Ingredients

4 whole wheat pita pockets

1 cup hummus (store-bought or homemade)

2 cups mixed salad greens (such as spinach, romaine, or arugula)

1 medium cucumber, thinly sliced

1 medium bell pepper (any color), thinly sliced

1 medium avocado, pitted, peeled, and thinly sliced

1/2 cup shredded carrots

1/2 cup alfalfa sprouts

Optional: your choice of protein (such as grilled chicken, turkey, tofu, or falafel)

Salt and pepper, to taste

Instructions

1. Cut the whole wheat pita pockets in half and gently open each half to create a pocket.

2. Spread a generous layer of hummus inside each pita pocket half.

3. Stuff the pita pockets with mixed salad greens, cucumber slices, bell pepper slices, avocado slices, shredded carrots, and alfalfa sprouts. If desired, add your choice of protein to the sandwich.

4. Season the sandwich filling with salt and pepper, to taste.

5. Serve the Veggie-Packed Whole Wheat Pita Sandwiches immediately, or wrap them in foil or plastic wrap and refrigerate for up to 2 hours before serving.

Turkey, Avocado, and Quinoa Bowl

 Serving(s): 04

 Preparing: 15 mins

 Cooking: 25-30 mins

Nutrients
(per serving, without optional toppings)

Calories: 510	Carbohydrates: 46g
Protein: 35g	Fiber: 8g
Fat: 22g	Sugar: 4g

The Turkey, Avocado, and Quinoa Bowl is a delicious and nutritious meal option, perfect for those following the Met Flex Diet or anyone looking for a balanced, protein-packed dish. Combining lean ground turkey, creamy avocado, fiber-rich quinoa, and a variety of fresh vegetables, this bowl is full of flavor and nutrients, making it a great choice for a satisfying and healthy meal.

Ingredients

1 cup uncooked quinoa

2 cups water or low-sodium chicken broth

1 pound lean ground turkey

1 tbsp olive oil

1/2 cup diced onion

1/2 cup diced bell pepper (any color)

1/2 cup cherry tomatoes, halved

1 medium avocado, pitted, peeled, and diced

1/2 cup chopped fresh cilantro

1 lime, juiced

Salt and pepper, to taste

Optional toppings: salsa, hot sauce, or Greek yogurt

Instructions

1. Rinse the quinoa in a fine mesh strainer under cold water. In a medium saucepan, bring the 2 cups of water or chicken broth to a boil. Add the rinsed quinoa, reduce the heat to low, cover, and simmer for 15-20 minutes, or until the quinoa is tender and the liquid is absorbed. Remove from heat and let it stand for 5 minutes. Fluff with a fork and set aside.

2. In a large skillet, heat the olive oil over medium-high heat. Add the ground turkey and cook, breaking it apart with a spatula, until fully cooked and no longer pink, about 5-7 minutes. Remove the cooked turkey from the skillet and set aside.

3. In the same skillet, add the diced onion and bell pepper. Cook, stirring frequently, for 5-7 minutes, or until the vegetables are tender and lightly browned.

4. In a large bowl, combine the cooked quinoa, cooked ground turkey, sautéed onion and bell pepper, halved cherry tomatoes, diced avocado, and chopped cilantro. Drizzle the lime juice over the mixture and toss gently to combine.

5. Season the Turkey, Avocado, and Quinoa Bowl with salt and pepper, to taste. Serve warm or chilled, with optional toppings such as salsa, hot sauce, or Greek yogurt.

Grilled Vegetable and Chickpea Salad

 Serving(s): 04

 Preparing: 15 mins

 Cooking: 10-14 mins

Nutrients
(per serving)

Calories: 300	Carbohydrates: 34g
Protein: 9g	Fiber: 9g
Fat: 16g	Sugar: 10g

The Grilled Vegetable and Chickpea Salad is a delicious and nutritious meal option, perfect for those following the Met Flex Diet or anyone looking for a balanced, fiber-rich dish. Combining a variety of grilled vegetables, protein-packed chickpeas, and a zesty lemon dressing, this salad is full of flavor and nutrients, making it a great choice for a satisfying and healthy meal.

Ingredients

1 medium zucchini, sliced into 1/4-inch rounds

1 medium yellow squash, sliced into 1/4-inch rounds

1 medium bell pepper (any color), cut into 1-inch pieces

1 medium red onion, cut into 1-inch pieces

2 cups cherry tomatoes

1 15-ounce can chickpeas, drained and rinsed

1/4 cup olive oil, divided

Salt and pepper, to taste

2 tbsps freshly squeezed lemon juice

1 tbsp red wine vinegar

1 tsp honey or maple syrup

1/2 tsp Dijon mustard

1/4 cup chopped fresh parsley

Instructions

1. Preheat a grill or grill pan to medium-high heat. In a large bowl, toss the zucchini, yellow squash, bell pepper, red onion, and cherry tomatoes with 2 tablespoons of olive oil. Season the vegetables with salt and pepper, to taste.

2. Grill the vegetables in a grill basket or on skewers for 5-7 minutes per side, or until they are tender and have grill marks. Alternatively, you can use a grill pan on the stovetop. Remove the vegetables from the grill and let them cool slightly.

3. In a small bowl, whisk together the remaining 2 tablespoons of olive oil, lemon juice, red wine vinegar, honey or maple syrup, and Dijon mustard. Season the dressing with salt and pepper, to taste.

4. In a large salad bowl, combine the grilled vegetables, chickpeas, and chopped parsley. Drizzle the lemon dressing over the salad and toss gently to combine. Adjust seasoning with salt and pepper, if necessary.

5. Serve the Grilled Vegetable and Chickpea Salad warm or chilled.

Sweet Potato and Black Bean Burrito Bowl

 Serving(s): 04

 Preparing: 15 mins

 Cooking: 30-35 mins

Nutrients
(per serving, without optional toppings)

Calories: 495	Carbohydrates: 78g
Protein: 14g	Fiber: 15g
Fat: 16g	Sugar: 10g

The Sweet Potato and Black Bean Burrito Bowl is a delicious and nutritious meal option, perfect for those following the Met Flex Diet or anyone looking for a balanced, fiber-rich dish. Combining tender roasted sweet potatoes, protein-packed black beans, and a variety of fresh vegetables and toppings, this bowl is full of flavor and nutrients, making it a great choice for a satisfying and healthy meal.

Ingredients

2 large sweet potatoes, peeled and diced into 1/2-inch cubes
2 tbsps olive oil, divided
Salt and pepper, to taste
1 15-ounce can black beans, drained and rinsed
2 cups cooked brown rice or quinoa
1 cup corn kernels, fresh or thawed from frozen
1 cup cherry tomatoes, halved
1 medium avocado, pitted, peeled, and diced
1/4 cup chopped fresh cilantro
1 lime, juiced
Optional toppings: salsa, hot sauce, Greek yogurt, or shredded cheese

Instructions

1. Preheat the oven to 400°F (200°C). In a large bowl, toss the diced sweet potatoes with 1 tablespoon of olive oil. Season with salt and pepper, to taste. Spread the sweet potatoes in a single layer on a baking sheet lined with parchment paper or a silicone baking mat. Roast for 25-30 minutes, or until tender and lightly browned, stirring halfway through the cooking time. Remove from the oven and let cool slightly.

2. In a large skillet, heat the remaining 1 tablespoon of olive oil over medium heat. Add the black beans and cook, stirring occasionally, for 3-4 minutes, or until heated through. Season with salt and pepper, to taste.

3. To assemble the burrito bowls, divide the cooked brown rice or quinoa among 4 serving bowls. Top each bowl with equal portions of roasted sweet potatoes, black beans, corn kernels, cherry tomatoes, diced avocado, and chopped cilantro.

4. Drizzle the lime juice over each bowl and season with additional salt and pepper, if desired. Serve the Sweet Potato and Black Bean Burrito Bowls with optional toppings such as salsa, hot sauce, Greek yogurt, or shredded cheese.

Soba Noodle Salad with Edamame

 Serving(s): 04   **Preparing:** 15 mins   **Cooking:** 10-12 mins

Nutrients
(per serving, without optional toppings)

Calories: 350	Carbohydrates: 57g
Protein: 18g	Fiber: 6g
Fat: 8g	Sugar: 10g

The Soba Noodle Salad with Edamame is a delicious and nutritious meal option, perfect for those following the Met Flex Diet or anyone looking for a balanced, fiber-rich dish. Combining nutty soba noodles, protein-packed edamame, and a variety of fresh vegetables and toppings, this salad is full of flavor and nutrients, making it a great choice for a satisfying and healthy meal.

Ingredients

8 ounces soba noodles (buckwheat noodles)

2 cups shelled edamame, fresh or thawed from frozen

1 medium red bell pepper, thinly sliced

1 medium carrot, julienned or shredded

2 green onions, thinly sliced

1/4 cup chopped fresh cilantro

1/4 cup soy sauce or tamari

2 tbsps rice vinegar

1 tbsp sesame oil

1 tbsp honey or maple syrup

1 tsp grated fresh ginger

1 clove garlic, minced

Optional toppings: sesame seeds, chopped peanuts, or cashews

Instructions

1. Bring a large pot of water to a boil. Cook the soba noodles according to the package instructions, adding the edamame during the last 3-4 minutes of cooking time. Drain the noodles and edamame, then rinse under cold water to stop the cooking process and remove any excess starch.

2. In a large salad bowl, combine the cooked soba noodles and edamame, red bell pepper, carrot, green onions, and chopped cilantro.

3. In a small bowl, whisk together the soy sauce or tamari, rice vinegar, sesame oil, honey or maple syrup, grated ginger, and minced garlic. Pour the dressing over the soba noodle salad and toss gently to combine.

4. Serve the Soba Noodle Salad with Edamame immediately, or refrigerate for at least 1 hour to let the flavors meld. Garnish with optional toppings such as sesame seeds, chopped peanuts, or cashews before serving.

Chapter 06
Dinner
Recipes

*15 Mouth-watering
Dinner Recipes*

TABLE OF CONTENTS

Baked Lemon Herb Salmon

 Serving(s): 04   **Preparing:** 10 mins   **Cooking:** 12-15 mins

The combination of tender, flaky salmon with the bright flavors of lemon and fresh herbs makes for a satisfying and healthy meal. Serve this dish with your favorite side of vegetables, grains, or salad for a complete meal experience.

Nutrients (per serving)

Calories: 350   Carbohydrates: 3g

Protein: 34g   Fiber: 1g

Fat: 21g   Sugar: 1g

HIGH-PROTEIN

Ingredients

4 salmon fillets, 6 ounces each, skin on

Salt and pepper, to taste

2 tbsps olive oil

2 cloves garlic, minced

Zest and juice of 1 lemon

1 tbsp chopped fresh parsley

1 tbsp chopped fresh dill

1 tbsp chopped fresh chives

Optional garnish: lemon wedges and additional chopped herbs

Instructions

1. Preheat the oven to 400°F (200°C). Line a baking sheet with parchment paper or aluminum foil.
2. Pat the salmon fillets dry with paper towels and season both sides with salt and pepper. Place the fillets skin-side-down on the prepared baking sheet, spaced evenly apart.
3. In a small bowl, combine the olive oil, minced garlic, lemon zest, and lemon juice. Brush the mixture evenly over the tops of the salmon fillets.
4. In another small bowl, mix together the chopped parsley, dill, and chives. Sprinkle the herb mixture over the salmon fillets, pressing gently to adhere.
5. Bake the salmon in the preheated oven for 12-15 minutes, or until the salmon is cooked through and flakes easily with a fork. The internal temperature should reach 145°F (63°C) when measured with a meat thermometer.
6. Remove the salmon from the oven and let it rest for a couple of minutes before serving. Garnish with additional lemon wedges and chopped herbs, if desired.

Chicken and Vegetable Skewers

 Serving(s): 04   **Preparing:** 20 mins   **Cooking:** 10-12 mins

Marinated in a simple and delicious sauce, the chicken becomes tender and juicy, while the grilled vegetables add a delightful smoky flavor. Serve these skewers with your favorite side dishes, such as rice, quinoa, or salad, for a complete and satisfying meal.

Nutrients (per serving)

Calories: 320

Carbohydrates: 16g

Protein: 35g

Fiber: 2g

Fat: 12g

Sugar: 11g

HIGH-PROTEIN

Ingredients

1 1/2 pounds boneless, skinless chicken breasts, cut into 1-inch cubes

1/4 cup olive oil

3 tbsps soy sauce or tamari

2 tbsps honey or maple syrup

1 tbsp lemon juice

2 cloves garlic, minced

Salt and pepper, to taste

1 bell pepper, cut into 1-inch pieces

1 red onion, cut into 1-inch pieces

1 zucchini, cut into 1/2-inch thick slices

1 pint cherry tomatoes

8 wooden or metal skewers

Instructions

1. In a medium bowl, whisk together the olive oil, soy sauce or tamari, honey or maple syrup, lemon juice, minced garlic, salt, and pepper. Add the chicken cubes to the marinade, making sure each piece is well coated. Cover and refrigerate for at least 1 hour or up to overnight for the best flavor.

2. If using wooden skewers, soak them in water for at least 30 minutes to prevent burning during grilling.

3. Preheat the grill or grill pan to medium-high heat.

4. Thread the marinated chicken and vegetables onto the skewers, alternating between chicken, bell pepper, red onion, zucchini, and cherry tomatoes. Discard any remaining marinade.

5. Grill the skewers for 10-12 minutes, turning occasionally, until the chicken is cooked through and the vegetables are tender with a slight char. The internal temperature of the chicken should reach 165°F (74°C) when measured with a meat thermometer.

6. Remove the skewers from the grill and let them rest for a few minutes before serving.

Turkey Meatballs with Marinara Sauce

 Serving(s): 04   **Preparing:** 15 mins   **Cooking:** 15-40 mins

These tender and flavorful meatballs are made with lean ground turkey, providing a healthy and satisfying alternative to traditional beef meatballs. Serve the turkey meatballs over your favorite pasta, spaghetti squash, or zucchini noodles for a complete and delicious meal.

Nutrients (per serving)

Calories: 320

Carbohydrates: 18g

Protein: 28g

Fiber: 3g

Fat: 12g

Sugar: 6g

HIGH-PROTEIN

Ingredients

1 pound lean ground turkey

1/2 cup breadcrumbs

1/4 cup grated Parmesan cheese

1/4 cup chopped fresh parsley

1/4 cup finely chopped onion

2 cloves garlic, minced

1 large egg, lightly beaten

Salt and pepper, to taste

2 tbsps olive oil

3 cups marinara sauce, store-bought or homemade

Optional garnish: additional grated Parmesan cheese and chopped fresh parsley

Instructions

1. In a large bowl, combine the ground turkey, breadcrumbs, Parmesan cheese, chopped parsley, chopped onion, minced garlic, beaten egg, salt, and pepper. Mix until all the ingredients are well incorporated, but avoid overmixing to keep the meatballs tender.

2. Shape the mixture into 1 1/2-inch meatballs, forming approximately 16-18 meatballs.

3. Heat the olive oil in a large skillet over medium heat. Add the meatballs in a single layer, working in batches if necessary. Cook the meatballs for 6-8 minutes, turning occasionally, until they are browned on all sides.

4. Remove the meatballs from the skillet and set them aside. Pour off any excess oil from the skillet.

5. Add the marinara sauce to the skillet and bring it to a simmer. Carefully return the meatballs to the skillet, nestling them into the sauce. Cover the skillet and let the meatballs simmer in the sauce for 20-25 minutes, or until they are cooked through and the internal temperature reaches 165°F (74°C) when measured with a meat thermometer.

6. Serve the Turkey Meatballs with Marinara Sauce over your choice of pasta, spaghetti squash, or zucchini noodles. Garnish with additional grated Parmesan cheese and chopped fresh parsley, if desired.

Seared Tuna Steaks

 Serving(s): 04

 Preparing: 5 mins

 Cooking: 5-6 mins

These tender, flavorful steaks are quickly seared to preserve their natural texture, while the simple seasoning highlights the tuna's natural flavors. Serve the seared tuna steaks with your favorite side dishes, such as steamed vegetables, quinoa, or a fresh salad for a complete and satisfying meal.

Nutrients (per serving)

Calories: 230

Carbohydrates: 0g

Protein: 40g

Fiber: 0g

Fat: 8g

Sugar: 0g

HIGH-PROTEIN

Ingredients

4 tuna steaks, 6 ounces each, about 1-inch thick

Salt and pepper, to taste

1 tsp olive oil

1 tsp sesame oil

Optional garnish: sesame seeds, chopped fresh cilantro, and lime wedges

Instructions

1. Remove the tuna steaks from the refrigerator and let them sit at room temperature for 10-15 minutes before cooking.
2. Pat the tuna steaks dry with paper towels and season both sides with salt and pepper.
3. In a large skillet, heat the olive oil and sesame oil over medium-high heat until shimmering but not smoking.
4. Carefully add the tuna steaks to the skillet in a single layer, making sure they do not touch. Cook the steaks for 2-3 minutes per side for medium-rare, or until they reach the desired level of doneness. Adjust the cooking time depending on the thickness of the steaks and your personal preference.
5. Remove the seared tuna steaks from the skillet and let them rest for a couple of minutes before slicing or serving.
6. If desired, garnish the tuna steaks with sesame seeds, chopped fresh cilantro, and lime wedges.

Chickpea and Spinach Curry

 Serving(s): 04   **Preparing:** 10 mins   **Cooking:** 30 mins

This vegan curry is packed with hearty chickpeas, tender spinach, and a rich, aromatic blend of spices. Serve this Chickpea and Spinach Curry over brown rice, quinoa, or with warm naan bread for a complete and satisfying meal.

Nutrients (per serving)

Calories: 365

Carbohydrates: 45g

Protein: 15g

Fiber: 12g

Fat: 15g

Sugar: 10g

HIGH-PROTEIN

Ingredients

2 tbsps coconut oil or vegetable oil
1 large onion, finely chopped
3 cloves garlic, minced
1-inch piece of ginger, grated
1 tbsp garam masala
1 tsp ground cumin
1 tsp ground coriander
1/2 tsp turmeric
1/4 tsp cayenne pepper (optional)

1/2 tsp paprika
Salt, to taste
1 (14.5-ounce) can diced tomatoes, with their juices
2 (15-ounce) cans chickpeas, drained and rinsed
1 cup vegetable broth or water
4 cups fresh spinach, roughly chopped
1/2 cup canned coconut milk or yogurt
Optional garnish: chopped fresh cilantro and lime wedges

Instructions

1. In a large pot or deep skillet, heat the coconut oil or vegetable oil over medium heat. Add the chopped onion and cook for 5-7 minutes, or until softened and slightly golden.
2. Add the minced garlic and grated ginger to the pot and cook for 1 minute, stirring constantly to prevent burning.
3. Add the garam masala, ground cumin, ground coriander, turmeric, paprika, cayenne pepper (if using), and salt to the pot. Cook for 1-2 minutes, stirring constantly, until the spices are fragrant.
4. Stir in the diced tomatoes with their juices, chickpeas, and vegetable broth or water. Bring the mixture to a simmer and let it cook for 10-15 minutes, stirring occasionally, until the flavors meld and the curry thickens slightly.
5. Stir in the chopped spinach and cook for an additional 3-4 minutes, or until the spinach has wilted and is fully incorporated into the curry.
6. Remove the pot from the heat and stir in the coconut milk or yogurt to create a creamy, rich sauce.
7. Taste the curry and adjust the seasoning with additional salt or spices, if needed.
8. Serve the Chickpea and Spinach Curry over your choice of brown rice, quinoa, or with warm naan bread. Garnish with chopped fresh cilantro and lime wedges, if desired.

Eggplant Parmesan

 Serving(s): 06   **Preparing:** 60 mins   **Cooking:** 30 mins

This delicious and nutritious meal option is perfect for those following the Met Flex Diet or anyone looking for a balanced, protein-rich dish. Serve this Eggplant Parmesan with a side of whole wheat pasta, spaghetti squash, or a green salad for a complete and satisfying meal.

Nutrients (per serving)

Calories: 480   Carbohydrates: 45g

Protein: 22g   Fiber: 8g

Fat: 25g   Sugar: 12g

LOW-CARB

Ingredients

2 large eggplants, sliced into 1/2-inch thick rounds
Salt, for drawing out moisture from eggplant slices
1 cup all-purpose flour
2 large eggs, lightly beaten
2 cups breadcrumbs (preferably Italian-seasoned)
1/2 cup grated Parmesan cheese
1 tsp dried basil
1 tsp dried oregano
Freshly ground black pepper, to taste
1/4 cup olive oil, divided
3 cups marinara sauce, store-bought or homemade
2 cups shredded mozzarella cheese
Optional garnish: additional grated Parmesan cheese and chopped fresh basil

Instructions

1. Lay the eggplant slices on a large baking sheet and sprinkle both sides generously with salt. Let them sit for 30-45 minutes to draw out the moisture. Rinse the eggplant slices under cold water to remove the salt and pat them dry with paper towels.
2. Preheat your oven to 375°F (190°C) and prepare a large baking sheet with parchment paper.
3. Set up a breading station: Place the flour, beaten eggs, and breadcrumbs in three separate shallow dishes. Mix the Parmesan cheese, dried basil, dried oregano, and black pepper into the breadcrumbs.
4. Dredge each eggplant slice in flour, then dip it into the beaten eggs, and finally coat it with the breadcrumb mixture. Place the breaded eggplant slices on the prepared baking sheet in a single layer.
5. Heat 2 tablespoons of olive oil in a large skillet over medium heat. Working in batches, fry the breaded eggplant slices for 2-3 minutes per side, or until golden brown. Add more oil as needed between batches.
6. In a 9x13-inch baking dish, spread 1 cup of marinara sauce on the bottom. Layer half of the fried eggplant slices over the sauce, followed by another cup of marinara sauce and half of the shredded mozzarella cheese. Repeat the layers with the remaining eggplant slices, marinara sauce, and mozzarella cheese.
7. Bake the Eggplant Parmesan in the preheated oven for 25-30 minutes, or until the cheese is melted and bubbly.
8. Remove the Eggplant Parmesan from the oven and let it rest for a few minutes before serving. Garnish with additional grated Parmesan cheese and chopped fresh basil, if desired.

Stuffed Portobello Mushrooms

 Serving(s): 06   **Preparing:** 20 mins   **Cooking:** 20 mins

These tender, meaty mushrooms are filled with a savory mixture of vegetables, cheese, and herbs, making for a satisfying and flavorful meal. Serve the Stuffed Portobello Mushrooms with a side of mixed greens, quinoa, or roasted vegetables for a complete and wholesome dining experience.

Nutrients (per serving)

Calories: 250

Carbohydrates: 20g

Protein: 12g

Fiber: 3g

Fat: 14g

Sugar: 6g

LOW-CARB

Ingredients

6 large portobello mushroom caps, stems removed and gills scraped out

2 tbsps olive oil, divided

Salt and pepper, to taste

1 small onion, finely chopped

2 cloves garlic, minced

1 cup finely chopped bell pepper (any color)

1 cup finely chopped zucchini

1/2 cup breadcrumbs (preferably whole wheat)

1/2 cup grated Parmesan cheese

1/4 cup chopped fresh parsley

1/4 cup chopped fresh basil

1 cup shredded mozzarella cheese

Instructions

1. Preheat your oven to 375°F (190°C) and line a baking sheet with parchment paper or aluminum foil.
2. Brush the portobello mushroom caps with 1 tablespoon of olive oil and season them with salt and pepper. Place the mushroom caps, gill-side up, on the prepared baking sheet.
3. In a large skillet, heat the remaining 1 tablespoon of olive oil over medium heat. Add the chopped onion and cook for 4-5 minutes, or until softened.
4. Add the minced garlic, chopped bell pepper, and chopped zucchini to the skillet. Cook for another 5-6 minutes, or until the vegetables are tender.
5. Remove the skillet from the heat and stir in the breadcrumbs, Parmesan cheese, chopped parsley, and chopped basil. Season the mixture with salt and pepper, to taste.
6. Divide the vegetable mixture evenly among the portobello mushroom caps, pressing it firmly into the caps.
7. Top each stuffed mushroom with a generous amount of shredded mozzarella cheese.
8. Bake the Stuffed Portobello Mushrooms in the preheated oven for 15-20 minutes, or until the mushrooms are tender and the cheese is melted and bubbly.
9. Remove the mushrooms from the oven and let them cool for a few minutes before serving.

Beef and Broccoli Stir-Fry

 Serving(s): 04   **Preparing:** 15 mins   **Cooking:** 15 mins

This protein-rich, balanced meal option is perfect for those following the Met Flex Diet or anyone looking for a quick and satisfying dinner. Serve this Beef and Broccoli Stir-Fry over brown rice, quinoa, or cauliflower rice for a complete and wholesome meal.

Nutrients (per serving)

Calories: 295

Carbohydrates: 15g

Protein: 28g

Fiber: 2g

Fat: 13g

Sugar: 8g

LOW-CARB

Ingredients

1 pound flank steak, thinly sliced against the grain

1/4 cup soy sauce, divided

1 tbsp cornstarch

3 tbsps vegetable oil, divided

4 cups broccoli florets

1/2 cup water

1/4 cup oyster sauce

2 tbsps brown sugar

1 tbsp minced garlic

1 tsp minced ginger

1/2 tsp crushed red pepper flakes (optional)

Instructions

1. In a medium bowl, combine the thinly sliced flank steak with 2 tablespoons of soy sauce and the cornstarch. Toss to coat the beef evenly and set aside to marinate for 10-15 minutes.
2. In a large skillet or wok, heat 2 tablespoons of vegetable oil over medium-high heat. Add the marinated beef and stir-fry for 2-3 minutes, or until browned and cooked through. Remove the beef from the skillet and set it aside on a plate.
3. In the same skillet, add the remaining 1 tablespoon of vegetable oil and the broccoli florets. Stir-fry the broccoli for 2-3 minutes, then add the water and cover the skillet. Cook for another 3-4 minutes, or until the broccoli is crisp-tender.
4. While the broccoli cooks, prepare the sauce by mixing the remaining 2 tablespoons of soy sauce, oyster sauce, brown sugar, minced garlic, minced ginger, and crushed red pepper flakes (if using) in a small bowl.
5. Add the cooked beef back into the skillet with the broccoli, and pour the sauce over the top. Stir-fry everything together for 1-2 minutes, or until the sauce thickens and coats the beef and broccoli evenly.
6. Remove the skillet from the heat and serve the Beef and Broccoli Stir-Fry immediately over your choice of brown rice, quinoa, or cauliflower rice.

Spaghetti Squash Carbonara

  Serving(s): 04 **Preparing:** 20 mins **Cooking:** 45 mins

By swapping traditional pasta with tender strands of spaghetti squash, this dish becomes lighter and more nutrient-dense, while still offering the creamy, comforting flavors of traditional carbonara. Perfect for those following the Met Flex Diet, this protein-rich meal option is sure to become a favorite in your recipe repertoire.

Nutrients (per serving)

Calories: 420

Carbohydrates: 18g

Protein: 20g

Fiber: 4g

Fat: 31g

Sugar: 8g

LOW-CARB

Ingredients

1 large spaghetti squash (about 3-4 pounds)

1 tbsp olive oil

Salt and pepper, to taste

8 ounces pancetta or bacon, diced

1 small onion, finely chopped

2 cloves garlic, minced

3 large eggs, lightly beaten

1 cup grated Parmesan cheese

1/4 cup chopped fresh parsley

Optional: crushed red pepper flakes, to taste

Instructions

1. Preheat your oven to 400°F (200°C) and line a baking sheet with parchment paper or aluminum foil.
2. Cut the spaghetti squash in half lengthwise and remove the seeds. Drizzle the cut sides with olive oil and season with salt and pepper. Place the squash halves cut-side down on the prepared baking sheet.
3. Bake the spaghetti squash in the preheated oven for 30-40 minutes, or until the flesh is tender and can be easily scraped with a fork into spaghetti-like strands. Remove the squash from the oven and let it cool for a few minutes before using a fork to scrape out the strands. Set the strands aside.
4. In a large skillet, cook the diced pancetta or bacon over medium heat until crisp. Remove the cooked pancetta from the skillet with a slotted spoon and set it aside on a plate.
5. In the same skillet with the rendered pancetta fat, cook the chopped onion for 4-5 minutes, or until softened. Add the minced garlic and cook for an additional 1-2 minutes, or until fragrant.
6. In a medium bowl, whisk together the beaten eggs and grated Parmesan cheese.
7. Reduce the skillet heat to low and add the cooked spaghetti squash strands, tossing to combine with the onion and garlic mixture. Slowly pour in the egg and cheese mixture, stirring constantly to ensure the eggs don't scramble. The residual heat from the squash and skillet will cook the eggs and create a creamy sauce.
8. Add the cooked pancetta back into the skillet and mix well. Season with salt and pepper, to taste, and add crushed red pepper flakes if desired.
9. Remove the skillet from the heat and stir in the chopped fresh parsley.
10. Serve the Spaghetti Squash Carbonara immediately, garnishing with additional Parmesan cheese and parsley if desired.

Chicken Fajita Bowls

 Serving(s): 04   **Preparing:** 20 mins   **Cooking:** 15 mins

Packed with protein and fiber, these bowls are perfect for those following the Met Flex Diet or anyone looking for a satisfying and balanced lunch or dinner. You can easily customize the Chicken Fajita Bowls with your favorite toppings, grains, or vegetables for a personalized meal experience.

Nutrients (per serving)

Calories: 350	Carbohydrates: 40g
Protein: 30g	Fiber: 5g
Fat: 8g	Sugar: 4g

LOW-CARB

Ingredients

1 pound boneless, skinless chicken breasts, thinly sliced
1 tbsp olive oil
1 tbsp chili powder
1 tsp ground cumin
1 tsp paprika
1/2 tsp onion powder
1/2 tsp garlic powder
Salt and pepper, to taste
1 red bell pepper, thinly sliced
1 yellow bell pepper, thinly sliced
1 onion, thinly sliced
2 cups cooked brown rice or quinoa
Optional toppings: avocado, salsa, shredded cheese, sour cream, chopped cilantro, lime wedges

Instructions

1. In a medium bowl, combine the sliced chicken breasts with the olive oil, chili powder, ground cumin, paprika, onion powder, garlic powder, salt, and pepper. Toss to coat the chicken evenly and set aside to marinate for at least 10 minutes.

2. In a large skillet, heat an additional tablespoon of olive oil over medium heat. Add the marinated chicken to the skillet and cook for 5-6 minutes, or until browned and cooked through. Remove the cooked chicken from the skillet and set it aside on a plate.

3. In the same skillet, add the thinly sliced bell peppers and onion. Cook the vegetables for 5-6 minutes, or until they are tender and slightly charred.

4. Add the cooked chicken back into the skillet with the vegetables and stir to combine.

5. To assemble the Chicken Fajita Bowls, divide the cooked brown rice or quinoa among four serving bowls. Top each bowl with an equal portion of the chicken and vegetable mixture.

6. Serve the Chicken Fajita Bowls with your choice of toppings, such as avocado, salsa, shredded cheese, sour cream, chopped cilantro, and lime wedges.

Shrimp and Vegetable Quinoa Stir-Fry

 Serving(s): 04   **Preparing:** 15 mins   **Cooking:** 20 mins

This versatile recipe is perfect for those following the Met Flex Diet or anyone looking for a quick and healthy lunch or dinner. Feel free to customize the Shrimp and Vegetable Quinoa Stir-Fry with your favorite vegetables, protein, or sauce for a personalized meal experience.

Nutrients (per serving)

Calories: 400 kcal

Carbohydrates: 45 g

Protein: 30 g

Fiber: 6 g

Fat: 10 g

Sugar: 8 g

BALANCED

Ingredients

1 cup uncooked quinoa

2 cups water

Salt and pepper, to taste

1 pound large shrimp, peeled and deveined

2 tbsps olive oil, divided

1 small onion, diced

1 red bell pepper, chopped

1 yellow bell pepper, chopped

1 zucchini, chopped

1 cup snap peas, trimmed

3 cloves garlic, minced

1/4 cup soy sauce

1 tbsp honey

1 tbsp fresh lime juice

Optional: chopped cilantro, green onions, sesame seeds

Instructions

1. Rinse the quinoa under cold water in a fine-mesh strainer. In a medium saucepan, combine the rinsed quinoa, water, and a pinch of salt. Bring the mixture to a boil, then reduce the heat to low and cover the saucepan. Simmer the quinoa for 15 minutes, or until the water is absorbed and the quinoa is tender. Remove the saucepan from the heat and let it stand, covered, for 5 minutes before fluffing the quinoa with a fork.

2. Season the shrimp with salt and pepper. In a large skillet or wok, heat 1 tablespoon of olive oil over medium-high heat. Add the shrimp and cook for 2-3 minutes per side, or until pink and cooked through. Remove the cooked shrimp from the skillet and set it aside on a plate.

3. In the same skillet, heat the remaining 1 tablespoon of olive oil. Add the diced onion and cook for 2-3 minutes, or until softened. Add the chopped bell peppers, zucchini, and snap peas, and cook for an additional 5-6 minutes, or until the vegetables are tender-crisp.

4. Stir in the minced garlic and cook for 1 minute, or until fragrant.

5. In a small bowl, whisk together the soy sauce, honey, and lime juice. Pour the sauce over the cooked vegetables in the skillet, and then add the cooked shrimp and quinoa. Stir to combine everything and heat through.

6. Serve the Shrimp and Vegetable Quinoa Stir-Fry immediately, garnishing with optional toppings like chopped cilantro, green onions, or sesame seeds if desired.

Lentil and Vegetable Stuffed Peppers

 Serving(s): 04

 Preparing: 20 mins

 Cooking: 40 mins

This vegetarian dish is perfect for those following the Met Flex Diet or anyone looking for a satisfying and nutrient-dense lunch or dinner. Feel free to customize the Lentil and Vegetable Stuffed Peppers with your favorite vegetables, spices, or grains for a personalized meal experience.

Nutrients (per serving)

Calories: 300

Carbohydrates: 50g

Protein: 15g

Fiber: 12g

Fat: 6g

Sugar: 8g

BALANCED

Ingredients

4 large bell peppers (any color), halved and seeds removed

1 tbsp olive oil

1 small onion, diced

2 cloves garlic, minced

1 cup cooked green or brown lentils

1 cup cooked quinoa or rice

1 cup chopped tomatoes

1 cup corn kernels (fresh or frozen)

1 cup black beans, drained and rinsed

1 tsp ground cumin

1/2 tsp smoked paprika

Salt and pepper, to taste

Optional toppings: shredded cheese, avocado, sour cream, chopped cilantro, hot sauce

Instructions

1. Preheat your oven to 375°F (190°C) and lightly grease a large baking dish.
2. In a large skillet, heat the olive oil over medium heat. Add the diced onion and cook for 3-4 minutes, or until softened. Stir in the minced garlic and cook for an additional 1 minute, or until fragrant.
3. Add the cooked lentils, quinoa or rice, chopped tomatoes, corn kernels, black beans, ground cumin, and smoked paprika to the skillet. Season with salt and pepper, to taste. Cook the mixture for 5-6 minutes, or until the vegetables are tender and the flavors have melded together.
4. Place the halved bell peppers cut-side up in the prepared baking dish. Spoon the lentil and vegetable mixture evenly into each pepper half.
5. Cover the baking dish with aluminum foil and bake the stuffed peppers for 30-35 minutes, or until the peppers are tender and the filling is heated through.
6. Remove the foil and, if desired, sprinkle the stuffed peppers with shredded cheese. Return the baking dish to the oven and bake for an additional 5 minutes, or until the cheese is melted and bubbly.
7. Serve the Lentil and Vegetable Stuffed Peppers hot, with optional toppings like avocado, sour cream, chopped cilantro, or hot sauce if desired.

Roasted Chicken and Root Vegetables

 Serving(s): 04   **Preparing:** 20 mins   **Cooking:** 60-75 mins

This one-pan dish is perfect for those following the Met Flex Diet or anyone looking for a delicious and well-balanced lunch or dinner. The versatile recipe allows you to customize the Roasted Chicken and Root Vegetables with your favorite seasonings, herbs, or vegetables for a personalized meal experience.

Nutrients (per serving)

Calories: 450

Carbohydrates: 29g

Protein: 30g

Fiber: 7g

Fat: 24g

Sugar: 9g

BALANCED

Ingredients

1 whole chicken (3-4 pounds),
giblets removed and patted dry
Salt and pepper, to taste
2 tbsps olive oil, divided
1 tbsp unsalted butter, softened
2 tsps fresh thyme leaves, chopped
2 tsps fresh rosemary, chopped
4 medium carrots, peeled and chopped into 1-inch pieces
4 medium parsnips, peeled and chopped into 1-inch pieces
2 medium turnips, peeled and chopped into 1-inch pieces
1 large onion, cut into wedges
3 cloves garlic, minced
Optional: fresh parsley, chopped, for garnish

Instructions

1. Preheat your oven to 425°F (220°C) and position a rack in the lower third of the oven.
2. Season the chicken cavity generously with salt and pepper. Tie the legs together with kitchen twine and tuck the wing tips under the body of the chicken.
3. In a small bowl, combine 1 tablespoon of olive oil, the softened butter, chopped thyme, and chopped rosemary. Rub the herb butter mixture all over the chicken, making sure to coat the breast and legs evenly.
4. In a large bowl, toss the chopped carrots, parsnips, turnips, onion wedges, and minced garlic with the remaining 1 tablespoon of olive oil. Season the vegetables with salt and pepper, to taste.
5. Spread the seasoned root vegetables in an even layer on a large rimmed baking sheet or roasting pan. Place the seasoned chicken on top of the vegetables.
6. Roast the chicken and vegetables for 60-75 minutes, or until the internal temperature of the chicken reaches 165°F (74°C) when measured at the thickest part of the thigh. Stir the vegetables occasionally to ensure even cooking and browning.
7. Remove the roasted chicken and vegetables from the oven and let the chicken rest for 10-15 minutes before carving.
8. Serve the carved roasted chicken with the root vegetables, garnished with chopped fresh parsley if desired.

Chickpea and Vegetable Couscous

 Serving(s): 04   **Preparing:** 15 mins   **Cooking:** 15 mins

This vegetarian dish is perfect for those following the Met Flex Diet or anyone looking for a quick and nutrient-dense lunch or dinner. The versatile recipe allows you to customize the Chickpea and Vegetable Couscous with your favorite vegetables, spices, or grains for a personalized meal experience.

Nutrients (per serving)

Calories: 340

Carbohydrates: 60g

Protein: 13g

Fiber: 9g

Fat: 6g

Sugar: 6g

BALANCED

Ingredients

1 cup uncooked couscous
1 1/4 cups water or vegetable broth
1 tbsp olive oil
1 small onion, diced
2 cloves garlic, minced
1 medium zucchini, chopped
1 medium red bell pepper, chopped
1 medium yellow bell pepper, chopped
1 1/2 cups cooked chickpeas
(or one 15-ounce can, drained and rinsed)
1 tsp ground cumin
1/2 tsp ground turmeric
1/2 tsp paprika
Salt and pepper, to taste
1/4 cup chopped fresh parsley
1/4 cup chopped fresh cilantro
Juice of 1 lemon

Instructions

1. In a medium saucepan, bring the water or vegetable broth to a boil. Stir in the couscous, cover the saucepan, and remove it from the heat. Let the couscous stand for 5 minutes, or until the liquid is absorbed. Fluff the couscous with a fork and set it aside.

2. In a large skillet, heat the olive oil over medium heat. Add the diced onion and cook for 3-4 minutes, or until softened. Stir in the minced garlic and cook for an additional 1 minute, or until fragrant.

3. Add the chopped zucchini, red bell pepper, and yellow bell pepper to the skillet. Cook the vegetables for 5-6 minutes, or until they are tender-crisp.

4. Stir in the cooked chickpeas, ground cumin, ground turmeric, and paprika. Season the mixture with salt and pepper, to taste. Cook the chickpea and vegetable mixture for an additional 3-4 minutes, or until heated through.

5. Add the cooked couscous to the skillet and stir to combine everything evenly. Remove the skillet from the heat and stir in the chopped fresh parsley, chopped fresh cilantro, and lemon juice.

6. Serve the Chickpea and Vegetable Couscous warm, garnished with additional fresh herbs if desired.

Turkey Chili

 Serving(s): 04   **Preparing:** 15 mins   **Cooking:** 45-60 mins

This healthy and filling dish is perfect for those following the Met Flex Diet or anyone looking for a satisfying and nutrient-dense lunch or dinner. The versatile recipe allows you to customize the Turkey Chili with your favorite beans, vegetables, spices, or toppings for a personalized meal experience.

Nutrients (per serving)

Calories: 410 kcal

Carbohydrates: 42 g

Protein: 35 g

Fiber: 14 g

Fat: 12 g

Sugar: 9 g

BALANCED

Ingredients

1 tbsp olive oil

1 pound lean ground turkey

1 medium onion, diced

2 cloves garlic, minced

1 medium red bell pepper, diced

1 medium green bell pepper, diced

1 jalapeño pepper, seeded and minced (optional, for heat)

1 (28-ounce) can crushed tomatoes

1 (15-ounce) can black beans, drained and rinsed

1 (15-ounce) can kidney beans, drained and rinsed

1 cup low-sodium chicken or vegetable broth

1 tbsp chili powder

1 tbsp ground cumin

1/2 tbsp smoked paprika

Salt and pepper, to taste

Optional toppings: shredded cheese, sour cream, chopped green onions, chopped cilantro, avocado

Instructions

1. In a large pot or Dutch oven, heat the olive oil over medium heat. Add the ground turkey and cook, breaking it up with a spoon, until browned and cooked through. Remove the cooked turkey from the pot and set it aside.
2. In the same pot, add the diced onion and cook for 3-4 minutes, or until softened. Stir in the minced garlic and cook for an additional 1 minute, or until fragrant.
3. Add the diced red and green bell peppers and minced jalapeño (if using) to the pot. Cook the vegetables for 5-6 minutes, or until they are tender.
4. Stir in the cooked ground turkey, crushed tomatoes, black beans, kidney beans, chicken or vegetable broth, chili powder, ground cumin, and smoked paprika. Season the chili with salt and pepper, to taste.
5. Bring the chili to a boil, then reduce the heat to low and let it simmer for 30-45 minutes, or until the flavors have melded together and the chili has thickened to your desired consistency.
6. Serve the Turkey Chili hot, topped with your choice of optional toppings like shredded cheese, sour cream, chopped green onions, chopped cilantro, or avocado.

Chapter 07

Snacks

Recipes

15 Mouth-watering Snacks Recipes

TABLE OF CONTENTS

Greek Yogurt with Honey and Walnuts

Greek Yogurt with Honey and Walnuts is a simple yet delicious breakfast or snack option that combines creamy Greek yogurt with the natural sweetness of honey and the crunch of nutrient-rich walnuts.

Preparation Time : 5 mins

Cooking Time : 0 min

Servings : 01

HIGH-PROTEIN

Ingredients

1 cup plain Greek yogurt (preferably 2% fat)

2 tbsps honey

1/3 cup walnuts, roughly chopped

Optional: fresh berries or fruit for serving

Instructions

1. In a bowl, combine the Greek yogurt with 1 tablespoon of honey and mix until well combined.
2. Transfer the Greek yogurt mixture to a serving bowl or individual bowls.
3. Drizzle the remaining 1 tablespoon of honey over the Greek yogurt.
4. Sprinkle the roughly chopped walnuts on top of the yogurt.
5. If desired, add fresh berries or fruit of your choice to the Greek Yogurt with Honey and Walnuts before serving.

Nutrients (per serving)

Calories: 410

Protein: 20g

Fat: 26g

Carbohydrates: 29g

Fiber: 2g

Sugar: 26g

Edamame

Edamame, or young soybeans, are a popular and nutritious snack or side dish that can be enjoyed steamed, boiled, or even roasted.

Preparation Time : 5 mins

Cooking Time : 5 min

Servings : 02

HIGH-PROTEIN

Nutrients (per serving)

Calories: 190

Protein: 17g

Fat: 8g

Carbohydrates: 14g

Fiber: 8g

Sugar: 3g

Ingredients

2 cups frozen edamame in pods

Water, for boiling

1/2 tbsp sea salt or kosher salt, plus more for serving

Optional seasonings: garlic powder, onion powder, red pepper flakes, lemon zest, or sesame seeds

Instructions

1. Bring a large pot of water to a boil. While waiting for the water to boil, fill a large bowl with ice water and set it aside.
2. Once the water is boiling, add the frozen edamame and 1/2 teaspoon of salt to the pot. Cook the edamame for 3-5 minutes, or until the beans are tender but still bright green.
3. Use a slotted spoon to transfer the cooked edamame to the ice water bath. This will help to stop the cooking process and preserve the vibrant green color of the beans.
4. After the edamame has cooled for about 1 minute, drain the beans and pat them dry with a clean kitchen towel or paper towels.
5. Transfer the cooked and cooled edamame to a serving bowl. If desired, toss the beans with your choice of optional seasonings like garlic powder, onion powder, red pepper flakes, lemon zest, or sesame seeds.
6. Serve the edamame immediately, sprinkled with additional sea salt or kosher salt if desired. Enjoy the beans by squeezing the pods to release the tender beans inside.

Cottage Cheese and Sliced Peaches

Cottage Cheese and Sliced Peaches is a light and refreshing breakfast or snack option that pairs creamy, protein-rich cottage cheese with the natural sweetness of ripe peaches.

Preparation Time : 5 mins

Cooking Time : N/A

Servings : 01

HIGH-PROTEIN

Ingredients

1 cup low-fat cottage cheese

1 medium ripe peach, pitted and sliced

Optional toppings: honey, cinnamon, toasted almonds, or granola

Instructions

1. Place the low-fat cottage cheese in a serving bowl or individual bowls.
2. Arrange the sliced peaches on top of the cottage cheese.
3. If desired, drizzle with honey, sprinkle with cinnamon, and/or add other toppings like toasted almonds or granola before serving.

Nutrients (per serving)

Calories: 210

Protein: 26g

Fat: 2g

Carbohydrates: 20g

Fiber: 2g

Sugar: 17g

Turkey Roll-Ups

This versatile and portable recipe is perfect for those following the Met Flex Diet or anyone seeking a low-carb alternative to traditional sandwiches.

Preparation Time : 10 mins

Cooking Time : N/A

Servings : 02 (02 roll-ups/serving)

HIGH-PROTEIN

Nutrients (per serving)

Calories: 280

Protein: 23g

Fat: 18g

Carbohydrates: 5g

Fiber: 2g

Sugar: 1g

Ingredients

4 slices of low-sodium deli turkey (preferably oven-roasted or smoked)

4 tsps whole grain mustard or your favorite spread

4 slices of Swiss cheese or your preferred cheese

1/2 avocado, thinly sliced

1/2 small cucumber, thinly sliced

Optional additions: baby spinach, bell pepper strips, thinly sliced red onion

Instructions

1. Lay the turkey slices on a clean work surface or cutting board. Spread 1 teaspoon of whole grain mustard or your favorite spread onto each slice of turkey.

2. Place a slice of Swiss cheese or your preferred cheese on top of each turkey slice.

3. Divide the avocado and cucumber slices evenly among the turkey slices, arranging them along the center of each slice. If desired, add other ingredients like baby spinach, bell pepper strips, or thinly sliced red onion.

4. Roll each turkey slice tightly around the fillings, securing with a toothpick if necessary.

5. Cut the Turkey Roll-Ups in half, if desired, or leave them whole. Serve immediately or refrigerate until ready to enjoy.

Protein Energy Bites

These no-bake energy bites combine rolled oats, nut butter, protein powder, and other wholesome ingredients to create a satisfying treat that can be customized with your favorite mix-ins.

Preparation Time : 10 mins

Cooking Time : N/A

Servings : 20

HIGH-PROTEIN

Nutrients (per serving)

Calories: 120 kcal

Protein: 6 g

Fat: 6 g

Carbohydrates: 12 g

Fiber: 2 g

Sugar: 6 g

Ingredients

1 cup rolled oats

1/2 cup natural nut butter (such as almond, peanut, or cashew butter)

1/3 cup honey or maple syrup

1/2 cup vanilla or chocolate protein powder

1/4 cup ground flaxseed

1/4 cup unsweetened shredded coconut

Optional mix-ins: mini chocolate chips, chopped nuts, dried fruit, or chia seeds

Instructions

1. In a large bowl, combine the rolled oats, nut butter, honey or maple syrup, protein powder, ground flaxseed, and shredded coconut. Mix until all ingredients are well incorporated.

2. If desired, add your choice of optional mix-ins like mini chocolate chips, chopped nuts, dried fruit, or chia seeds, and mix until evenly distributed throughout the mixture.

3. Using a cookie scoop or your hands, form the mixture into small balls, each about the size of a golf ball. Place the formed Protein Energy Bites onto a parchment-lined baking sheet or plate.

4. Refrigerate the Protein Energy Bites for at least 30 minutes, or until they are firm and hold their shape.

5. Store the Protein Energy Bites in an airtight container in the refrigerator for up to 1 week, or freeze them for longer storage.

Celery Sticks with Almond Butter

Celery Sticks with Almond Butter is a simple and nutritious snack that combines the satisfying crunch of celery with the rich creaminess of almond butter.

Preparation Time : 5 mins

Cooking Time : N/A

Servings : 04 (03-4 sticks/serving)

LOW-CARB

Nutrients (per serving)

Calories: 90

Protein: 3g

Fat: 7g

Carbohydrates: 4g

Fiber: 2g

Sugar: 1g

Ingredients

4 large celery stalks, washed and trimmed

1/4 cup natural almond butter, or your preferred nut or seed butter

Optional toppings: raisins, dried cranberries, chia seeds, or hemp seeds

Instructions

1. Cut the celery stalks into 3-4 inch long pieces, resulting in about 12-16 celery sticks.

2. Spread a thin layer of almond butter onto the concave side of each celery stick, filling the natural groove.

3. If desired, sprinkle the celery sticks with your choice of optional toppings like raisins, dried cranberries, chia seeds, or hemp seeds.

4. Arrange the Celery Sticks with Almond Butter on a plate or platter and serve immediately, or refrigerate until ready to enjoy.

Parmesan Crisps

Made with just one ingredient—Parmesan cheese—these crisps are perfect for those following the Met Flex Diet or anyone seeking a gluten-free alternative to traditional chips or crackers.

Preparation Time : 5 mins

Cooking Time : 5-7 mins

Servings : 08 (2 crisps/serving)

LOW-CARB

Ingredients

1 cup finely grated Parmesan cheese

Instructions

1. Preheat your oven to 350°F (175°C) and line a large baking sheet with parchment paper or a silicone baking mat.

2. Using a tablespoon measure or a small cookie scoop, place small mounds of grated Parmesan cheese onto the prepared baking sheet, spacing them about 2 inches apart.

3. Use your fingers or the back of a spoon to gently flatten each mound of cheese into a thin, even circle, approximately 2 inches in diameter.

4. Bake the Parmesan Crisps in the preheated oven for 5-7 minutes, or until the edges are golden brown and the cheese is bubbly.

5. Remove the baking sheet from the oven and allow the Parmesan Crisps to cool for a few minutes on the baking sheet. Then, use a spatula to transfer the crisps to a wire rack to cool completely and firm up.

6. Store the cooled Parmesan Crisps in an airtight container at room temperature for up to 1 week.

Nutrients (per serving)

Calories: 60

Protein: 6g

Fat: 4g

Carbohydrates: 1g

Fiber: 0g

Sugar: 0g

Cucumber and Smoked Salmon

Perfect for those following the Met Flex Diet or anyone seeking a low-carb, protein-packed option, this simple dish can be served at gatherings or enjoyed as a satisfying snack.

Preparation Time : 10 mins

Cooking Time : 5 mins

Servings : 04 (3-4 topped slices/serving)

LOW-CARB

Nutrients (per serving)

Calories: 70

Protein: 10g

Fat: 2g

Carbohydrates: 2g

Fiber: 1g

Sugar: 1g

Ingredients

1 large cucumber, washed and ends trimmed

4 oz smoked salmon, thinly sliced

1/4 cup cream cheese or Greek yogurt (optional)

Optional garnishes: fresh dill, capers, lemon wedges, cracked black pepper

Instructions

1. Using a sharp knife or a mandoline slicer, cut the cucumber into thin, even slices, about 1/8-inch thick.

2. Arrange the cucumber slices on a serving platter or plate.

3. If desired, spread a thin layer of cream cheese or Greek yogurt onto each cucumber slice.

4. Top each cucumber slice with a small piece of smoked salmon, folding or rolling the salmon to fit neatly on top of the cucumber.

5. If desired, garnish the Cucumber and Smoked Salmon with your choice of optional garnishes, such as fresh dill, capers, lemon wedges, or cracked black pepper.

6. Serve the Cucumber and Smoked Salmon immediately, or refrigerate until ready to enjoy.

Mini Caprese Salad Skewers

Perfect for those following the Met Flex Diet or anyone seeking a low-carb, nutrient-dense option, these skewers are ideal for serving at gatherings or enjoying as a refreshing snack.

Preparation Time : 15 mins

Cooking Time : N/A

Servings : 08 (2-3 skewers/serving)

LOW-CARB

Nutrients (per serving)

Calories: 100

Protein: 6g

Fat: 7g

Carbohydrates: 3g

Fiber: 1g

Sugar: 1g

Ingredients

1 pint cherry or grape tomatoes

8 oz small fresh mozzarella balls (bocconcini)

1/4 cup fresh basil leaves

Extra virgin olive oil, for drizzling

Balsamic glaze or reduction, for drizzling

Salt and freshly ground black pepper, to taste

Toothpicks or small skewers

Instructions

1. Wash and dry the cherry or grape tomatoes and basil leaves.

2. Assemble the Mini Caprese Salad Skewers by threading a cherry or grape tomato, a basil leaf (folded in half if large), and a mozzarella ball onto a toothpick or small skewer. Repeat with the remaining ingredients until all skewers are assembled.

3. Arrange the assembled Mini Caprese Salad Skewers on a serving platter or plate.

4. Drizzle the skewers with a small amount of extra virgin olive oil and balsamic glaze or reduction.

5. Season the Mini Caprese Salad Skewers with a pinch of salt and freshly ground black pepper, to taste.

6. Serve the Mini Caprese Salad Skewers immediately or refrigerate until ready to enjoy.

Olives and Feta Cheese

Perfect for those following the Met Flex Diet or anyone seeking a low-carb, nutrient-dense option, this dish is ideal for serving at gatherings or enjoying as a satisfying snack.

Preparation Time : 5 mins

Cooking Time : N/A

Servings : 04

LOW-CARB

Nutrients (per serving)

Calories: 180

Protein: 5g

Fat: 17g

Carbohydrates: 2g

Fiber: 1g

Sugar: 1g

Ingredients

1 cup mixed olives (e.g., Kalamata, green, black)

1 cup cubed feta cheese

1/4 cup extra virgin olive oil

1/2 tbsp dried oregano or your preferred herbs

Optional accompaniments: cucumber slices, cherry tomatoes, whole grain crackers

Instructions

1. In a small bowl, combine the mixed olives, cubed feta cheese, extra virgin olive oil, and dried oregano or your preferred herbs.

2. Gently toss the ingredients together until the olives and feta cheese are evenly coated with the olive oil and herbs.

3. Transfer the Olives and Feta Cheese mixture to a serving bowl or plate.

4. If desired, serve the Olives and Feta Cheese with optional accompaniments such as cucumber slices, cherry tomatoes, or whole grain crackers.

5. Serve the Olives and Feta Cheese immediately or refrigerate until ready to enjoy.

Apple Slices with Peanut Butter

Perfect for those following the Met Flex Diet or anyone seeking a balanced, nutrient-dense option, this dish is ideal for enjoying as a quick and easy snack.

Preparation Time : 5 mins

Cooking Time : N/A

Servings : 02

BALANCED

Nutrients (per serving)

Calories: 180

Protein: 5g

Fat: 12g

Carbohydrates: 15g

Fiber: 3g

Sugar: 10g

Ingredients

1 large apple, washed and cored

1/4 cup peanut butter or your preferred nut butter

Optional toppings: chopped nuts, chia seeds, raisins, or dark chocolate chips

Instructions

1. Using a sharp knife or an apple slicer, cut the apple into even slices, about 1/4-inch thick.
2. Arrange the apple slices on a plate or serving platter.
3. Spoon the peanut butter or your preferred nut butter into a small bowl for dipping.
4. If desired, sprinkle your choice of optional toppings over the peanut butter or apple slices, such as chopped nuts, chia seeds, raisins, or dark chocolate chips.
5. Serve the Apple Slices with Peanut Butter immediately or refrigerate until ready to enjoy.

Veggie Sticks with Hummus

Perfect for those following the Met Flex Diet or anyone seeking a nutrient-dense, plant-based option, this dish is ideal for enjoying as a quick and easy snack.

Preparation Time : 15 mins

Cooking Time : N/A

Servings : 04

BALANCED

Nutrients (per serving)

Calories: 140

Protein: 5g

Fat: 8g

Carbohydrates: 14g

Fiber: 5g

Sugar: 5g

Ingredients

1 cup baby carrots

1 cup cherry tomatoes

1 cup sliced bell peppers (red, yellow, or green)

1 cup sliced cucumber

1 cup broccoli florets

1 cup cauliflower florets

1 cup store-bought or homemade hummus (your preferred flavor)

Instructions

1. Wash and dry all vegetables, and prepare them by cutting them into sticks or bite-sized pieces as needed.
2. Arrange the veggie sticks on a serving platter or plate.
3. Spoon the hummus into a small serving bowl or directly onto the serving platter.
4. Serve the Veggie Sticks with Hummus immediately or refrigerate until ready to enjoy.

Rice Cakes with Avocado

Rice Cakes with Avocado is a light and nutritious snack that combines the satisfying crunch of rice cakes with the creamy, healthy fats of avocado.

Preparation Time : 5 mins

Cooking Time : N/A

Servings : 02

BALANCED

Nutrients (per serving)

Calories: 140

Protein: 2g

Fat: 9g

Carbohydrates: 15g

Fiber: 4g

Sugar: 1g

Ingredients

4 rice cakes (your preferred flavor)

1 ripe avocado

Salt and freshly ground black pepper, to taste

Optional toppings: red pepper flakes, sesame seeds, sliced cherry tomatoes, or chopped fresh cilantro

Instructions

1. Peel and pit the ripe avocado, then transfer the flesh to a small bowl.
2. Using a fork, mash the avocado until it reaches your desired consistency. Season with salt and freshly ground black pepper, to taste.
3. Spread the mashed avocado evenly onto the rice cakes.
4. If desired, garnish the Rice Cakes with Avocado with your choice of optional toppings, such as red pepper flakes, sesame seeds, sliced cherry tomatoes, or chopped fresh cilantro.
5. Serve the Rice Cakes with Avocado immediately or refrigerate until ready to enjoy.

Roasted Chickpeas

Perfect for those following the Met Flex Diet or anyone seeking a healthy, nutrient-dense option, this dish is ideal for enjoying as a quick and easy snack.

Preparation Time : 5 mins

Cooking Time : 30 mins

Servings : 04

BALANCED

Nutrients (per serving)

Calories: 130

Protein: 5g

Fat: 5g

Carbohydrates: 16g

Fiber: 4g

Sugar: 3g

Ingredients

1 (15 oz) can chickpeas, drained, rinsed, and patted dry

1 tbsp olive oil

1/2 tbsp salt

1/4 tbsp black pepper

Optional seasonings: smoked paprika, garlic powder, cayenne pepper, ground cumin, or curry powder

Instructions

1. Preheat your oven to 400°F (200°C). Line a large baking sheet with parchment paper.

2. In a medium-sized mixing bowl, combine the chickpeas, olive oil, salt, and black pepper. Toss to coat the chickpeas evenly.

3. If desired, add your choice of optional seasonings, such as smoked paprika, garlic powder, cayenne pepper, ground cumin, or curry powder. Toss again to distribute the seasonings evenly.

4. Spread the seasoned chickpeas in a single layer on the prepared baking sheet.

5. Roast the chickpeas in the preheated oven for 25-30 minutes, or until golden brown and crispy. Be sure to shake the baking sheet every 10 minutes for even roasting.

6. Remove the Roasted Chickpeas from the oven and let them cool for a few minutes before serving.

Mixed Nuts and Dried Fruit

Perfect for those following the Met Flex Diet or anyone seeking a nutrient-dense, energy-boosting option, this dish is ideal for enjoying as a quick and easy snack.

Preparation Time : 5 mins

Cooking Time : N/A

Servings : 08

BALANCED

Ingredients

1 cup mixed nuts (almonds, cashews, pecans, walnuts, etc.)

1 cup mixed dried fruit (raisins, cranberries, apricots, cherries, etc.)

Optional: 1/4 cup dark chocolate chips or unsweetened coconut flakes

Instructions

1. In a medium-sized mixing bowl, combine the mixed nuts and mixed dried fruit.
2. If desired, add optional ingredients such as dark chocolate chips or unsweetened coconut flakes for additional flavor and texture.
3. Mix well to evenly distribute the ingredients.
4. Transfer the Mixed Nuts and Dried Fruit to an airtight container or divide into individual snack bags for portion control and easy on-the-go snacking.

Nutrients (per serving)

Calories: 200

Protein: 5g

Fat: 12g

Carbohydrates: 20g

Fiber: 3g

Sugar: 12g

Chapter 08

Desserts

Recipes

15 Mouth-watering
Desserts Recipes

TABLE OF CONTENTS

Chocolate Protein Pudding

 Serving(s): 02   **Preparing:** 5 mins   **Chilling:** 30 mins

Perfect for those following the Met Flex Diet or anyone seeking a nutrient-dense, dessert-like option, this dish is ideal for enjoying as a quick and easy snack.

Ingredients

1 cup Greek yogurt (plain or vanilla)

1 scoop chocolate protein powder (your preferred brand)

1 tbsp unsweetened cocoa powder

1 tbsp honey or maple syrup (optional, for added sweetness)

Optional toppings: fresh berries, chopped nuts, unsweetened coconut flakes, or dark chocolate chips

Nutrients (per serving)

Calories: 230

Protein: 28g

Fat: 4g

Carbohydrates: 20g

Fiber: 2g

Sugar: 15g

Instructions

1. In a medium-sized mixing bowl, combine the Greek yogurt, chocolate protein powder, and unsweetened cocoa powder. Mix well until smooth and thoroughly combined.

2. If desired, add honey or maple syrup for additional sweetness, and mix well to incorporate.

3. Transfer the Chocolate Protein Pudding to an airtight container and refrigerate for at least 30 minutes to thicken and chill.

4. Before serving, top the pudding with your choice of optional toppings, such as fresh berries, chopped nuts, unsweetened coconut flakes, or dark chocolate chips.

5. Serve the Chocolate Protein Pudding chilled and enjoy.

Protein-Packed Peanut Butter Cookies

 Serving(s): 18   **Preparing:** 10 mins   **Cooking:** 10-12 mins

Perfect for those following the Met Flex Diet or anyone seeking a nutrient-dense, dessert-like option, these cookies are ideal for enjoying as a quick and easy dessert.

Ingredients

1 cup natural peanut butter (creamy or crunchy)

1/4 cup honey or maple syrup

1 large egg

1 tsp vanilla extract

1/2 cup chocolate or vanilla protein powder (your preferred brand)

1/2 tsp baking soda

Optional: 1/4 cup dark chocolate chips or chopped nuts

Nutrients (per serving)

Calories: 130

Protein: 7g

Fat: 8g

Carbohydrates: 9g

Fiber: 1g

Sugar: 6g

Instructions

1. Preheat your oven to 350°F (175°C). Line a large baking sheet with parchment paper or a silicone baking mat.

2. In a medium-sized mixing bowl, combine the peanut butter, honey or maple syrup, egg, and vanilla extract. Mix well until smooth and thoroughly combined.

3. Add the protein powder and baking soda to the peanut butter mixture. Stir until a thick dough forms.

4. If desired, fold in optional ingredients such as dark chocolate chips or chopped nuts for additional flavor and texture.

5. Using a tablespoon or cookie scoop, portion out the dough onto the prepared baking sheet, spacing the cookies about 2 inches apart.

6. Flatten each cookie slightly with the back of a fork, creating a crisscross pattern on top.

7. Bake the cookies in the preheated oven for 10-12 minutes, or until the edges are lightly golden and the cookies are set.

8. Remove the Protein-Packed Peanut Butter Cookies from the oven and let them cool on the baking sheet for 5 minutes before transferring them to a wire rack to cool completely.

Cottage Cheese and Fruit Parfait

 Serving(s): 02   **Preparing:** 10 mins   **Cooking:** N/A

Perfect for those following the Met Flex Diet or anyone seeking a nutrient-dense, dessert-like option, this parfait is ideal for enjoying as a quick and easy snack or breakfast.

Ingredients

1 cup cottage cheese (low-fat or full-fat)

1 cup mixed fresh fruit (strawberries, blueberries, raspberries, kiwi, etc.)

1/4 cup granola or muesli (optional)

1 tbsp honey or maple syrup (optional, for added sweetness)

Optional toppings: chopped nuts, unsweetened coconut flakes, or chia seeds

Nutrients (per serving)

Calories: 220

Protein: 20g

Fat: 5g

Carbohydrates: 25g

Fiber: 3g

Sugar: 20g

Instructions

1. In a small bowl or glass, layer half of the cottage cheese at the bottom.

2. Add a layer of half of the mixed fresh fruit on top of the cottage cheese.

3. If desired, add a layer of granola or muesli for additional texture and crunch.

4. Repeat the layers, using the remaining cottage cheese and mixed fresh fruit.

5. If desired, drizzle honey or maple syrup over the top for added sweetness.

6. Top the parfait with your choice of optional toppings, such as chopped nuts, unsweetened coconut flakes, or chia seeds.

7. Serve the Cottage Cheese and Fruit Parfait immediately, or cover and refrigerate for up to 2 hours before serving.

Chocolate Protein Mug Cak

 Serving(s): 01   **Preparing:** 5 mins   **Cooking:** 1-2 mins

Perfect for those following the Met Flex Diet or anyone seeking a nutrient-dense, dessert-like option, this mug cake can be enjoyed as a guilt-free snack or post-workout treat.

Ingredients

2 tbsps chocolate protein powder (your preferred brand)

1 tbsp unsweetened cocoa powder

1/4 tsp baking powder

1 large egg

2 tbsps almond milk or any milk of your choice

1 tbsp unsweetened applesauce

1 tbsp maple syrup or honey (optional, for added sweetness)

Optional toppings: fresh berries, chopped nuts, unsweetened coconut flakes, or a dollop of Greek yogurt

Nutrients (per serving)

Calories: 200

Protein: 20g

Fat: 7g

Carbohydrates: 15g

Fiber: 3g

Sugar: 9g

Instructions

1. In a microwave-safe mug or small bowl, combine the chocolate protein powder, unsweetened cocoa powder, and baking powder. Mix well until all the dry ingredients are combined.

2. Add the egg, almond milk, and unsweetened applesauce to the dry ingredients. Mix well until a smooth batter is formed.

3. If desired, add maple syrup or honey for additional sweetness, and mix well to incorporate.

4. Microwave the mug cake on high for 60-90 seconds, depending on your microwave's power. The cake should be cooked through but still slightly moist in the center.

5. Carefully remove the mug from the microwave (it may be hot), and let it cool for a minute.

6. Top the Chocolate Protein Mug Cake with your choice of optional toppings, such as fresh berries, chopped nuts, unsweetened coconut flakes, or a dollop of Greek yogurt.

7. Enjoy the mug cake warm or at room temperature.

Greek Yogurt Bark

 Serving(s): 08   **Preparing:** 10 mins   **Chilling:** 04 hrs

Made with simple, wholesome ingredients, this bark is easy to prepare and can be customized with your favorite mix-ins and toppings.

Ingredients

2 cups Greek yogurt (low-fat or full-fat)

2 tbsps honey or maple syrup (optional, for added sweetness)

1 tsp vanilla extract (optional)

1/2 cup mixed fruit (fresh or frozen; e.g., berries, mango, kiwi)

1/4 cup chopped nuts (e.g., almonds, walnuts, pecans)

Optional mix-ins and toppings: unsweetened coconut flakes, chia seeds, flaxseeds, or dark chocolate chips

Nutrients (per serving)

Calories: 100

Protein: 8g

Fat: 4g

Carbohydrates: 8g

Fiber: 1g

Sugar: 6g

Instructions

1. Line a baking sheet or large, flat dish with parchment paper.
2. In a medium-sized mixing bowl, combine the Greek yogurt, honey or maple syrup (if using), and vanilla extract (if using). Mix well until smooth and thoroughly combined.
3. Spread the yogurt mixture evenly onto the parchment-lined baking sheet or dish, creating a layer that's about 1/4 inch thick.
4. Scatter the mixed fruit and chopped nuts over the yogurt layer, gently pressing them into the yogurt.
5. If desired, add your choice of optional mix-ins and toppings, such as unsweetened coconut flakes, chia seeds, flaxseeds, or dark chocolate chips.
6. Place the baking sheet or dish in the freezer for at least 4 hours, or until the Greek Yogurt Bark is completely frozen and firm.
7. Once frozen, remove the bark from the freezer and break it into pieces using your hands or a knife.
8. Store the Greek Yogurt Bark in an airtight container in the freezer for up to 2 months.

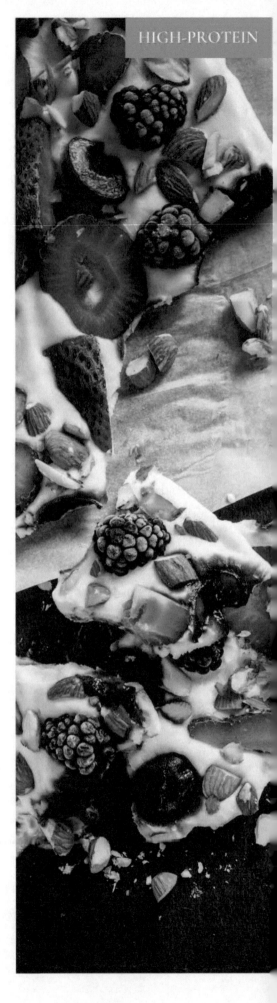

HIGH-PROTEIN

Keto Chocolate Mousse

 Serving(s): 04   **Preparing:** 15 mins   **Chilling:** 60 mins

Made with simple, wholesome ingredients, this bark is easy to prepare and can be customized with your favorite mix-ins and toppings.

Ingredients

1 cup heavy whipping cream

1/2 cup unsweetened cocoa powder

1/4 cup powdered erythritol or your preferred low-carb sweetener

1 tsp vanilla extract

Optional mix-ins and toppings: unsweetened coconut flakes, chopped nuts, dark chocolate chips, or fresh berries

Nutrients (per serving)

Calories: 250

Protein: 3g

Fat: 24g

Carbohydrates: 8g

Fiber: 4g

Sugar: 2g

Instructions

1. In a medium-sized mixing bowl, add the heavy whipping cream. Using an electric mixer or a whisk, whip the cream until soft peaks form.

2. In a separate bowl, combine the unsweetened cocoa powder and powdered erythritol or your preferred low-carb sweetener. Mix well to remove any lumps.

3. Gradually add the cocoa powder and sweetener mixture to the whipped cream, gently folding it in with a spatula until fully incorporated. Be careful not to deflate the whipped cream.

4. Add the vanilla extract to the mousse and fold it in gently until combined.

5. If desired, add your choice of optional mix-ins, such as unsweetened coconut flakes, chopped nuts, dark chocolate chips, or fresh berries.

6. Divide the Keto Chocolate Mousse evenly among 4 dessert cups or bowls.

7. Refrigerate the mousse for at least 1 hour to set before serving. If desired, garnish with your choice of toppings before enjoying.

Almond Flour Brownies

 Serving(s): 12   **Preparing:** 15 mins   **Cooking:** 20-25 mins

Almond Flour Brownies are a delicious, fudgy, and gluten-free alternative to traditional brownies, making them perfect for those following the Met Flex Diet or anyone seeking a nutritious treat.

Ingredients

1 1/2 cups almond flour
1/2 cup unsweetened cocoa powder
1/2 tsp baking powder
1/4 tsp salt
1 cup granulated sugar or your preferred sweetener
1/2 cup unsalted butter, melted and cooled
3 large eggs, room temperature
1 tsp vanilla extract
Optional mix-ins and toppings: chopped nuts, dark chocolate chips, or fresh berries

Nutrients (per serving)

Calories: 230

Protein: 6g

Fat: 17g

Carbohydrates: 17g

Fiber: 3g

Sugar: 12g

Instructions

1. Preheat your oven to 350°F (180°C) and line an 8x8-inch (20x20 cm) baking pan with parchment paper, allowing the paper to hang over the edges for easy removal.
2. In a medium-sized mixing bowl, combine the almond flour, unsweetened cocoa powder, baking powder, and salt. Mix well to combine and set aside.
3. In a separate mixing bowl, whisk together the granulated sugar (or preferred sweetener) and melted butter until smooth.
4. Add the eggs, one at a time, to the sugar and butter mixture, whisking well after each addition.
5. Stir in the vanilla extract.
6. Gradually add the almond flour mixture to the wet ingredients, stirring gently with a spatula until fully combined.
7. If desired, add your choice of optional mix-ins, such as chopped nuts, dark chocolate chips, or fresh berries.
8. Pour the brownie batter into the prepared baking pan, spreading it evenly with a spatula.
9. Bake the brownies for 20-25 minutes or until a toothpick inserted into the center comes out with a few moist crumbs attached. Be careful not to overbake, as this can cause the brownies to become dry.
10. Remove the pan from the oven and allow the brownies to cool completely in the pan before using the parchment paper to lift them out.
11. Cut the cooled brownies into squares and serve. Store any leftovers in an airtight container at room temperature for up to 5 days.

Coconut Macaroons

 Serving(s): 24

 Preparing: 15 mins

 Cooking: 20-25 mins

Coconut Macaroons are a delightful, chewy, and naturally gluten-free treat that is perfect for those following the Met Flex Diet or anyone seeking a delicious and easy-to-make dessert.

Ingredients

4 cups unsweetened shredded coconut

1 cup granulated sugar or your preferred sweetener

4 large egg whites, room temperature

1 tsp vanilla extract

1/4 tsp salt

Optional mix-ins and toppings: chocolate chips, chopped nuts, or a drizzle of melted dark chocolate

Nutrients (per serving)

Calories: 150

Protein: 2g

Fat: 12g

Carbohydrates: 10g

Fiber: 4g

Sugar: 6g

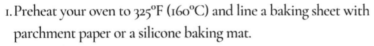

Instructions

1. Preheat your oven to 325°F (160°C) and line a baking sheet with parchment paper or a silicone baking mat.
2. In a medium-sized mixing bowl, combine the unsweetened shredded coconut, granulated sugar (or preferred sweetener), and salt. Mix well.
3. In a separate bowl, whisk the egg whites and vanilla extract until frothy.
4. Pour the frothy egg white mixture over the coconut mixture and gently fold with a spatula until fully combined.
5. If desired, add your choice of optional mix-ins, such as chocolate chips or chopped nuts.
6. Using a small cookie scoop or tablespoon, drop mounds of the coconut mixture onto the prepared baking sheet, spacing them about 1 inch (2.5 cm) apart.
7. Bake the coconut macaroons for 20-25 minutes or until the edges are golden brown and the tops are slightly toasted.
8. Remove the baking sheet from the oven and let the macaroons cool on the baking sheet for 5 minutes before transferring them to a wire rack to cool completely.
9. Once the macaroons have cooled, you can optionally drizzle them with melted dark chocolate for added flavor and visual appeal.
10. Store the cooled coconut macaroons in an airtight container at room temperature for up to 5 days.

Lemon Ricotta Cheesecake

 Serving(s): 12   **Preparing:** 20 mins   **Cooking:** 60-70 mins

Made with a combination of ricotta cheese and cream cheese, this cheesecake boasts a creamy texture and a bright lemon flavor.

Ingredients

1 1/2 cups almond flour
1/4 cup unsalted butter, melted
2 tbsps granulated sugar or your preferred sweetener (for the crust)
1/4 tsp salt
15 ounces ricotta cheese, drained
8 ounces cream cheese, room temperature
1 cup granulated sugar or your preferred sweetener (for the filling)
3 large eggs, room temperature
1/4 cup freshly squeezed lemon juice
1 tbsp lemon zest
1 tsp vanilla extract

Nutrients (per serving)

Calories: 280

Protein: 9g

Fat: 22g

Carbohydrates: 15g

Fiber: 1g

Sugar: 12g

Instructions

1. Preheat your oven to 325°F (160°C) and lightly grease a 9-inch (23 cm) springform pan.
2. In a medium-sized mixing bowl, combine the almond flour, melted butter, 2 tablespoons of granulated sugar (or preferred sweetener), and salt. Mix well until combined.
3. Press the almond flour mixture into the bottom of the prepared springform pan to form an even crust.
4. Bake the crust for 10 minutes, then remove it from the oven and let it cool while you prepare the filling.
5. In a large mixing bowl, beat the ricotta cheese and cream cheese together using an electric mixer on medium speed until smooth and well combined.
6. Gradually add the 1 cup of granulated sugar (or preferred sweetener) to the cheese mixture, continuing to beat until smooth.
7. Add the eggs, one at a time, to the cheese mixture, beating well after each addition.
8. Stir in the freshly squeezed lemon juice, lemon zest, and vanilla extract, mixing until fully combined.
9. Pour the filling over the cooled crust in the springform pan, smoothing the top with a spatula.
10. Bake the cheesecake for 60-70 minutes or until the edges are set, and the center is slightly jiggly but not wet.
11. Remove the cheesecake from the oven and let it cool to room temperature on a wire rack. Then, refrigerate the cheesecake for at least 4 hours or overnight to allow it to set completely.
12. Once the cheesecake has set, remove it from the springform pan, slice it into servings, and enjoy.

Chocolate Avocado Pudding

 Serving(s): 04   **Preparing:** 10 mins   **Cooking:** 60 mins

Made with ripe avocados, this pudding is packed with healthy fats and is naturally gluten-free and dairy-free.

Ingredients

2 ripe avocados, pitted and peeled

1/2 cup unsweetened cocoa powder

1/2 cup almond milk or any milk of your choice

1/3 cup pure maple syrup, honey, or your preferred sweetener

1 tsp vanilla extract

1/4 tsp sea salt

Optional toppings: fresh berries, coconut flakes, chopped nuts, or a dollop of whipped cream

Nutrients (per serving)

Calories: 200

Protein: 3g

Fat: 14g

Carbohydrates: 22g

Fiber: 7g

Sugar: 12g

LOW-CARB

Instructions

1. In a food processor or high-powered blender, combine the ripe avocados, unsweetened cocoa powder, almond milk, maple syrup (or preferred sweetener), vanilla extract, and sea salt.

2. Process or blend the ingredients until smooth and creamy, stopping to scrape down the sides of the container as needed. Adjust the sweetness to your taste if necessary.

3. Transfer the chocolate avocado pudding to serving bowls or ramekins, cover with plastic wrap, and refrigerate for at least 1 hour to allow the pudding to thicken and the flavors to meld.

4. When ready to serve, remove the pudding from the refrigerator and top with your choice of optional toppings, such as fresh berries, coconut flakes, chopped nuts, or a dollop of whipped cream.

5. Enjoy the chocolate avocado pudding chilled for a refreshing and nutrient-dense dessert.

Baked Cinnamon Apple Slices

 Serving(s): 04   **Preparing:** 10 mins   **Cooking:** 15-20 mins

Baked Cinnamon Apple Slices are a warm, flavorful, and healthy dessert that is perfect for those following the Met Flex Diet or anyone seeking a satisfying and guilt-free treat.

Ingredients

4 large apples, cored and sliced into thin wedges (choose your favorite variety, such as Granny Smith, Fuji, or Honeycrisp)

1 tbsp fresh lemon juice

2 tbsps granulated sugar or your preferred sweetener

1 tsp ground cinnamon

1/4 tsp ground nutmeg

Optional toppings: Greek yogurt, vanilla ice cream, or whipped cream

Nutrients (per serving)

Calories: 110

Protein: 1g

Fat: 0g

Carbohydrates: 29g

Fiber: 5g

Sugar: 22g

Instructions

1. Preheat your oven to 350°F (175°C) and line a large baking sheet with parchment paper.
2. In a large mixing bowl, toss the apple slices with the fresh lemon juice to prevent browning.
3. In a small bowl, combine the granulated sugar (or preferred sweetener), ground cinnamon, and ground nutmeg. Mix well to combine.
4. Sprinkle the sugar-cinnamon mixture over the apple slices and toss until the apples are evenly coated.
5. Arrange the apple slices in a single layer on the prepared baking sheet, ensuring that they do not overlap.
6. Bake the apple slices in the preheated oven for 15-20 minutes, or until the apples are tender and slightly caramelized.
7. Remove the baked apple slices from the oven and allow them to cool for a few minutes before serving.
8. Serve the baked cinnamon apple slices warm, topped with a dollop of Greek yogurt, a scoop of vanilla ice cream, or whipped cream, if desired.

BALANCED

Dark Chocolate-Dipped Strawberries

 Serving(s): 08   **Preparing:** 15 mins   **Cooking:** 15-30 mins

Dark Chocolate-Dipped Strawberries are a classic, elegant, and healthy dessert that is perfect for those following the Met Flex Diet or anyone seeking a satisfying and guilt-free treat.

BALANCED

Ingredients

1 pound fresh strawberries, rinsed and patted dry

8 ounces high-quality dark chocolate (70% cocoa or higher), chopped

Optional toppings: chopped nuts, unsweetened coconut flakes, or crushed freeze-dried berries

Nutrients (per serving)

Calories: 130

Protein: 2g

Fat: 7g

Carbohydrates: 16g

Fiber: 3g

Sugar: 11g

Instructions

1. Line a large baking sheet or tray with parchment paper or a silicone baking mat.
2. Prepare the optional toppings by placing them in small bowls, if using.
3. In a heatproof bowl, melt the chopped dark chocolate using a double boiler method or in the microwave. If using a double boiler, ensure that the bottom of the bowl does not touch the simmering water. If using a microwave, melt the chocolate in 30-second intervals, stirring between each interval, until the chocolate is completely melted and smooth.
4. Holding each strawberry by the stem or leaves, dip it into the melted dark chocolate, allowing the excess chocolate to drip back into the bowl.
5. If using optional toppings, immediately roll or sprinkle the chocolate-dipped strawberry with the desired topping.
6. Place the chocolate-dipped strawberry onto the prepared baking sheet or tray, and repeat with the remaining strawberries.
7. Allow the chocolate-dipped strawberries to set at room temperature or place them in the refrigerator for a faster setting time, about 15-30 minutes.
8. Once the chocolate has set, serve the dark chocolate-dipped strawberries immediately or store them in an airtight container in the refrigerator for up to 2 days.

Chia Seed and Berry Parfait

Serving(s): 04 **Preparing:** 15 mins **Cooking:** 02 hrs

Made with fiber-rich chia seeds, creamy yogurt, and antioxidant-packed berries, this parfait is both healthy and indulgent.

Ingredients

1/4 cup chia seeds

1 cup almond milk or milk of your choice

1 tbsp honey or sweetener of your choice

1 tsp vanilla extract

2 cups Greek yogurt or yogurt of your choice

2 cups mixed fresh berries (e.g., strawberries, blueberries, raspberries, blackberries)

Optional toppings: granola, chopped nuts, or unsweetened coconut flakes

Nutrients (per serving)

Calories: 210

Protein: 12g

Fat: 8g

Carbohydrates: 25g

Fiber: 7g

Sugar: 15g

Instructions

1. In a medium bowl, combine the chia seeds, almond milk (or milk of your choice), honey (or sweetener), and vanilla extract. Stir well to combine.

2. Cover the bowl with plastic wrap and refrigerate for at least 2 hours or overnight to allow the chia seeds to thicken and form a pudding-like consistency.

3. Once the chia seed mixture has thickened, begin assembling the parfaits. In a glass or jar, layer about 1/4 cup of the chia seed pudding, followed by 1/2 cup of Greek yogurt (or yogurt of your choice), and then 1/2 cup of mixed fresh berries.

4. Repeat the layering process until the glass or jar is full, finishing with a layer of fresh berries on top.

5. If desired, sprinkle the parfait with optional toppings such as granola, chopped nuts, or unsweetened coconut flakes.

6. Serve the chia seed and berry parfait immediately or refrigerate for up to 2 hours before serving.

Fruit Salad with Mint

 Serving(s): 04   **Preparing:** 15 mins   **Cooking:** 30 mins

Made with a variety of fresh, juicy fruits and a touch of aromatic mint, this fruit salad is both delicious and nutritious.

Ingredients

4 cups mixed fresh fruit, cut into bite-sized pieces (e.g., strawberries, pineapple, kiwi, grapes, blueberries, raspberries, mango)

1/4 cup freshly squeezed orange juice or lemon juice

1 tbsp honey or sweetener of your choice (optional)

1/4 cup fresh mint leaves, finely chopped

Optional garnish: additional fresh mint leaves

Nutrients (per serving)

Calories: 100

Protein: 1g

Fat: 0g

Carbohydrates: 25g

Fiber: 3g

Sugar: 18g

Instructions

1. In a large bowl, combine the mixed fresh fruit.

2. In a small bowl, whisk together the orange juice (or lemon juice), honey (or sweetener, if using), and finely chopped mint leaves.

3. Pour the mint mixture over the fruit, and gently toss to coat the fruit evenly.

4. Cover the bowl with plastic wrap and refrigerate the fruit salad for at least 30 minutes to allow the flavors to meld.

5. When ready to serve, give the fruit salad a gentle stir, and garnish with additional fresh mint leaves, if desired.

Oatmeal Raisin Cookies

 Serving(s): 24   *Preparing:* 15 mins   *Cooking:* 12-14 mins

Made with fiber-rich oats, plump raisins, and a touch of cinnamon, these cookies are both delicious and satisfying.

Ingredients

1 1/2 cups rolled oats

3/4 cup whole wheat flour

1/2 tsp baking soda

1/2 tsp cinnamon

1/4 tsp salt

1/2 cup unsweetened applesauce

1/4 cup coconut oil, melted

1/4 cup honey or maple syrup

1 large egg

1 tsp vanilla extract

3/4 cup raisins

Nutrients (per serving)

Calories: 90

Protein: 2g

Fat: 3g

Carbohydrates: 14g

Fiber: 1g

Sugar: 7g

Instructions

1. Preheat your oven to 350°F (180°C) and line a baking sheet with parchment paper or a silicone baking mat.

2. In a medium bowl, whisk together the rolled oats, whole wheat flour, baking soda, cinnamon, and salt.

3. In a separate large bowl, whisk together the unsweetened applesauce, melted coconut oil, honey (or maple syrup), egg, and vanilla extract until well combined.

4. Gradually add the dry ingredients to the wet ingredients, mixing until just combined.

5. Fold in the raisins until evenly distributed throughout the cookie dough.

6. Using a tablespoon or cookie scoop, drop rounded balls of dough onto the prepared baking sheet, spacing them about 2 inches apart.

7. Flatten the dough balls slightly with the back of a spoon or your fingertips.

8. Bake the cookies for 12-14 minutes, or until the edges are golden brown and the centers are set.

9. Allow the cookies to cool on the baking sheet for 5 minutes, then transfer them to a wire rack to cool completely.

19413506R00058